LEAVING
YOURSELF
BEHIND

An Inspirational Workbook for
Your Gifts to the Future

BY DALE BAILEY

INKWATER
PRESS

*Scan this QR Code
to learn more about
this title*

Cover and interior design by Emily Dueker
Drought © Yinghua. Dreamstime.com.
Author photo by Christie Martin Sando
Interior Photographs used with permission

Publisher:Inkwater Press|www.inkwaterpress.com

Spiral-bound
ISBN-13 978-1-59299-756-5 | ISBN-10 1-59299-756-2

Kindle
ISBN-13 978-1-59299-757-2 | ISBN-10 1-59299-757-0

Printed in the U.S.A.
All paper is acid free and meets all ANSI standards for archival quality paper.

1 3 5 7 9 10 8 6 4 2

Dedication

This book is dedicated to my mother

LOUELLA DOHERTY

Yakima Apple Blossom Princess – 1929

Her own giving nature inspired her family to endow a scholarship in her name.

CONTENTS

Acknowledgments

Readers of *Leaving Yourself Behind* will soon recognize that each chapter is a very personal acknowledgment of and tribute to people who have brought the birth of lasting legacies to fruition over the past 40 years in the Pacific Northwest. To fully give credit to the many contributors to this book and this region of the world that is now the center of philanthropy, please just read the stories.

However, these chronicles of dedication and sacrifice would never have been finished if it had not been for a small cadre of very special friends and family who gave this project their professional assistance and personal support.

Kristin Walker recognized her father's dream of helping others to find the beauty of leaving lasting legacies of love, and she personally inspired him to continue with writing this book. She even suggested adding a chapter called "Discover Your Caring Heart," then proceeded to compose the questionnaire.

Arliss Siebert is a former high school classmate at Elma, Washington. She has shared her editing and typing skills just in time to turn 15 years of sketchy notes and short stories into cohesive storylines and an overall idea whose time has come.

Michael Moore, outstanding professional proofreader, as well as multi-talented person, worked on this manuscript with a fine-tooth comb. If there are any errors, she pointed them out, but somehow the corrections didn't get completed.

Edward Schumacher is a nationally known and highly regarded fundraising consultant, teacher, and published author. Ed has always supported the mission to help people leave lasting legacies for their families and communities, and he graciously shared his publishing experience for this project.

Special thanks to David Hagiwara and his associate Holly Hairell at the port of Port Angeles, Washington. They shared historical documents which give full particulars regarding the gifting of waterfront property by Pilar and John Wayne for the purpose of establishing a public marina.

There are many others who have been very encouraging and supportive of this unique venture. Thank you for your own belief in leaving lasting legacies and for your personal efforts to make this world a better place for all.

LEAVING YOURSELF BEHIND

Quick look at the book - Overall purpose

"The future belongs to those who believe in
the beauty of their dreams."
–Eleanor Roosevelt (1884 - 1962)

Overall Purpose: To share very compelling and exciting true stories about people who, regardless of the size of their incomes or their estates, or even their state of health, have found ways to pass on the joy of giving to future generations by simply leaving lasting and measurable legacies of continuing support for their communities. There are also stories in this book that seem to confirm the theory that loving your neighbor as yourself is a principle that is cherished in most religions.

However, being inspired by other people's actions is only a portion of the purpose of this book. The real intention is to inspire action on the part of the reader. Therefore, this book also contains step-by-step instructions to establish lasting legacies for FAMILIES and for CHARITIES. Use the tested instructions, and you will be *Leaving Yourself Behind*.

One of the great mysteries of life is finding a magic formula to make it truly meaningful for you and me and others. Some of us

ALWAYS USE YOUR own attorney to execute your estate plan.

who have lived a long time are still looking to find ways to make a measurable and lasting difference to the communities where we live and, in some small way, help make the world a better place. With that intention the following chapters are presented to you.

IMAGINE A MEETING IN KING ARTHUR'S COURT

"The best way to suppose what may come is to
remember the past."
–Confucius (551-479 B.C.)

On a historic day under sunny skies in jolly old England in an exceptionally entertaining recent dream, some of the great philosophers of the ages came shuffling into a beautiful and ancient room that Leonardo Di Vinci had reserved at King Arthur's court. Some of the world's best minds began to take their seats at the same table where the Knights of the Roundtable had offered their wisdom and their courage to their fearless leader, King Arthur.

"How fitting," thought Plato, as he sat down right next to his fellow philosopher Aristotle. "How great to be back in England," said Winston Churchill, as Shakespeare was lighting Winston's very long cigar. Thoreau looked a little edgy; he wasn't sure he was in the right meeting. And Yogi Berra asked for the sports page while he sipped his coffee.

But in fact, every one of these great futurists was at exactly the right spot in the dream. Over the centuries, almost every great and caring philosopher had come to the same conclusion about God's mandate that we should leave the world and each community a far better place after our lifetime. Maybe these great philosophers could deliver a message so strong that the whole world would, at long last, realize that it's not the treasures that we pile up that count, but the treasures we leave behind for others.

Leonardo led off the meeting and got right to the point. "For thousands of years we have each espoused our own theories about the future and what mankind's contributions to the future should be. So now, for the entire world to hear, I want you to share once again the role mankind should play in the future of our world and the methods we can use to make our own lasting legacies a reality."

Thoreau stood immediately. "I have always said that we are only overseers of our estates. These material things are only ours to use not only for the successful lives of our families, but also our communities. To put it into 21st century terms...It ain't your money, so do something worthwhile with it."

The First Lady of the Broadway theater, Colleen Dewhurst, climbed right up on her feet on the subject of lasting legacies. "There was a reason my theater company, along with George C. Scott, brought the play Shadowbox to Broadway—a play about death and dying, which won both a Pulitzer Prize and a Toni Award because of its insight of death, not life."

Colleen now had their attention. "Three terminally ill cancer patients talk openly, and even humorously, about their impending demise and the process of dying. My favorite lines are when terminally ill Jack says to his friend Mark, 'And what do I have to show for my lifetime? What am I leaving behind? A refrigerator that ain't working, a long- term mortgage on my house with three equity loans, and a car payment. And if you think that's bad, look at my wife! What kind of legacy is this?'"

Winston Churchill was next on his feet, waving his cigar in the air as he did in Parliament. "I believe we all have a bit of destiny to fulfill. When I was named Prime Minister of Great Britain, everyone was shocked, including me, but over time I came to realize that I was the right man for the job. That was remarkable because I had lost so many men in the battle of Gallipoli, I could have been tarnished forever. But it didn't happen. I know that history will be good to me, for I plan to write it! My message: all men and women should write their own contributions to history."

As the meeting finally came to a close with a great plan to publish a full collection of the great observations of all our philosophers, it became crystal clear that Yogi Berra's simple observation about the future was the hit of the day.

When asked, Yogi simply said, "The future ain't what it used to be."

Chapter 1

CAN ONE PERSON MAKE A DIFFERENCE IN THE WORLD?

"The man who leaves money to charity in his will is
only giving away what no longer belongs to him."
–Voltaire (1694 - 1778)

One of the greatest mysteries of life is death. For thousands of years philosophers and pundits alike have been theorizing about death and possible/probable/hopes for a permanent place in heaven. But death has such finality that philosophers, historians and futurists continue to argue over whether death is the end or just the beginning of our immortality.

Richard Bach summarized it well when he said, "What the caterpillar calls the end of the world, the master calls a butterfly." James Barron Hope put it even more succinctly— "Tis after death that we measure men." Dewitt Wallace, who left us two great legacies, the *Reader's Digest* and the Dewitt Wallace Foundation, really meant it from the heart when he said, "The dead carry

1

with them to the grave in their clutched hands only that which they have given away."

The after-life that many religions promise fosters wonderful expectations for continued service to God and mankind from heaven, but quite often overlooks the importance of loving your neighbor as yourself not only while you are alive here, but ensuring that your neighbor will be better off even after you are gone! That is a lasting legacy instead of just a passing fancy.

The hope is that the real life examples in this book will illustrate that the greatest after-life imaginable is easily guaranteed when we stop looking at life for what we can do with our time and start looking at what our time here can do for future generations.

Some have called Jimmy and Rosalyn Carter the greatest postpresidential couple in U.S. history. Their investment of time and energy in worthwhile causes like Habitat for Humanity have easily given them permanent places in the hearts of the poor. As Rosalyn Carter has put it, "Every time I think I'm getting old and gradually going to the grave, something else happens." Perhaps it is just the beginning of the lasting legacies that every person can **IT IS A SAD STATISTIC** that only approximately 40% of Americans have a will, and of those who do, only 7% of them will leave a charitable bequest. and should leave behind. Being so involved in helping others guarantees that your life has continuing meaning.

People speak often about how fleeting their lives seem to be, and actually, when compared to all of man's recorded history, a lifetime is just a short blip on the screen. And yet, how precious a life can be, especially if you spend it in service to others and if it is filled with lasting legacies that will make life better for those who follow.

A GOOD DEFINITION

of a lasting legacy is a charitable bequest of $25,000 (or more) to set up a named and endowed fund (a permanent savings account) named for an honored member of your family.

One of the classic and true stories of all major gift fundraising is about the brilliant founder of a hardware company. It was tremendously successful as the direct result of the dynamic man who founded the company, named it for himself, and then built it (with his fantastic skills and financial expertise) into a national leader in its field. Later, he proudly left his legacy to a new ownership and management team, who would take the reigns. But only six months after he retired from his own company, the former CEO stopped by to see his old cronies at the office, only to discover that they had all retired shortly after he did, and the new receptionist did not even know his name because they had changed the name of the company.

It was not long after that lonely visit to his old company that the remarkable founder of his own hardware company was invited to be a visiting lecturer in the school of business of a local university. Within a year he was so engrossed in helping young people to understand the pitfalls of business (Don't sell your name.) and the thrill of business start-ups (Don't sell your name.), that he established several endowed business scholarships at the university and left a major gift in his will to have the business school named for him.

Hopefully, the lessons learned and the opportunities opened for almost anyone who wants to leave a lasting legacy are easy to spot in this oft-repeated scenario of losing a lasting legacy by default. Actually, lasting legacies are not hard to find if you know where to look and how easy it is to add one to your will.

Chapter 2

ALMOST ANYONE CAN LEAVE THEMSELVES BEHIND

"My interest is in the future because I'm
going to spend the rest of my life there!"
–Charles F. Kettering (1876 - 1958)

Finding ways to leave lasting legacies for future generations is a noble use of time and energy. If we look in earnest for affordable plans to actually leave lasting legacies behind, we can stretch our all-too-short life span into centuries of future worthwhile benefits. Once this has been done, many have found it is like discovering the fountain of youth.

Following are a few instances of how people have attained that goal. Please note that none of them are millionaires, but they did manage to leave a lasting legacy without a great deal of money.

HONORING A WAR HERO

A famous author in New York has enjoyed every possible joy that can come with writing that really makes a difference. Bob and his lovely wife are two of the greatest people one could imagine. Only one real sadness perseveres in Bob's life, and that is the early death of his brother in an ugly war. Now just imagine his pride each year when his brother's name is honored by a memorial fund that will keep his spirit alive forever.

DONATING A MATURED LIFE INSURANCE POLICY

A very young woman recently joined the staff of a highly successful charity program for the elderly in Seattle. One day she announced (with no fanfare) to her new boss that she had turned a $10,000 matured life insurance policy into an endowment gift to support the work of her new non-profit employer.

A CLASS ACTION GIFT BY ALUMNI

The high school graduating class of 1952 at Elma, Washington has left its own lasting legacy by establishing a permanent emergency student fund to cover unforeseen school expenditures that the families are not able to handle. Around the time for their annual reunion, they get details from the school principal regarding how the money is being used, preserving confidentiality, of course. At the class reunion that information is shared with all the classmates, so they know how the money given by their class has helped young people at their alma mater. Then they encourage the giving of new donations to replenish the fund. These former students take great pride in continuing their influence and assistance in helping the upcoming generation over some of the rough spots. It has been so successful that other classes are now contributing to the same fund.

ESTABLISHING THREE FUNDS WITH ONE GIFT

In early 2003 a woman passed away at age 102, leaving a very thoughtful bequest. Ten years previously, her daughter was dying and was helped by a Sisters of Providence hospice. Her end-of-life care was so exceptional, the mother established through her own will a permanently named endowment fund to honor her daughter and also provide an annual gift income for the hospice program.

Then, because the very elderly mother was so thankful for the care giver who helped her daughter progress from a very understandably stressful state to a very peaceful passing, the mother lovingly left a charitable trust in her will that pays an annual income for life to that very special care giver. So, all the hopes and dreams of that mother were realized in that one bequest:

1) Honoring her daughter with a permanently named endowed fund

2) Supporting the continuing work of the Sisters of Providence in their hospice care

3) Recognizing and rewarding the actual care giver who became a member of the family if only for 14 days of incredible service

All these permanent monuments of lasting legacies were rolled into one rather simple, but effective, charitable bequest, giving the mother and the daughter the very best kind of a permanent legacy.

Chapter 3

THESE PIONEERS IN PHILANTHROPY LED THE WAY IN THE PACIFIC NORTHWEST

*"The only thing we know about the future is
that it will be different."*
–Peter F. Drucker (1909-2005)

During the 19th and 20th centuries in the United States, there was very little doubt about which families were both wealthy and exceptionally benevolent. The great American pastime of giving to important community causes was actually birthed here in America by some of the richest families. Those families of John Rockefeller, Andrew Carnegie, Henry Ford, and Andrew Mellon are excellent case studies of this phenomenon called philanthropy.

The high-sounding word called philanthropy is actually well defined with the help of Greek root words. When it is broken down, *philo* means love, and anthropoid equates to man. So, there we have the "love of man", which is a fine definition for this wondrous virtue of community support. Alexis de Tocqueville acknowledged America's unique and revolutionary leadership in individual giving when he visited America in the 19th century. He was part of a special French mission to study our American forms of life and governance. Alexis de Tocqueville was astounded by our individual care for community causes and in his reports back to France made quite a point of acknowledging this "unique American tradition".

However, aside from the few above-named outstanding examples of benevolence, there was little wide-spread giving in America until the late 20th century. Leaving lasting legacies for favorite charities or community projects was generally not available or simply not done. But within the last one hundred years and especially the last 50 years, America has rightfully earned the title of the international birthplace of philanthropy. Then, in a very public display of America's joy in giving, Congress passed the very charity-supportive 1969 Tax Reform Act, with many brand-new deductions for charitable gifts. Congress even added new tax deductions for donor families who make future charitable gifts and trusts to charities.

Lately many Americans have begun to create their own permanent and lasting legacies by simply including their favorite charities in their wills. After their lifetimes the named family funds will be established. Others have achieved the same results with outright gifts. With this new emphasis on charitable giving, communities across the nation have established informational campaigns to emphasize both personal giving and volunteering for charitable causes.

The hallmark efforts of these early examples of true philanthropy in the Pacific Northwest were great works of art by wonderful community leaders, like the late Mary Gates, who chaired the first major capital campaign at Children's Hospital in 1975. At the turn of the century, Bill Gates, Sr. conceived and facilitated the visionary idea for the Bill and Melinda Gates Endowment Challenge Fund to largely reduce the operating costs of United Way of King County in support of 162 King County charities.

And then there were the Pigott family members, the Bullitt sisters, Jeff Brotman, and Shan Mullin...all early donors and volunteers.

These were also the years when many charities started new programs to attract gifts to the future, often called planned gifts. In 1971 the University of Puget Sound was funded by the Northwest Area Foundation to add to the staff a planned giving officer with estate planning expertise. A well-trained officer named Barry Smith left a major Seattle bank trust department to take the new position at the university and added over $2.5 million in endowment gifts to the future assets of the university in the first three years of his work.

About the same time an exceptionally well-trained estate planning PhD named Frank Minton was hired by the University of Washington to enhance their institutional endowment funds. Before Frank was done elevating planned giving at the University of Washington, he had already been chosen as the first recipient of the Development Officer of the Year Award, granted by the Northwest Development Officers Association. Frank later founded his own Seattle company called Planned Giving Services and has even assisted the Canadian government in modifications to the tax law that were more favorable for charitable giving.

However, the single most exciting breakthrough in Northwest philanthropy came in the mid-1970s when Children's Hospital in Seattle asked Mary Gates to chair the largest capital campaign ever attempted in the Northwest. The overall goal was set at $23,000,000, and very few leaders thought Children's Hospital could achieve it.

But Mary Gates, along with the Children's Hospital staff, conducted extensive internal research of the use of health services by various companies in the Puget Sound region. When Mary made her first call on the CEO of a major Pacific Northwest corporation, she brought the complete history of health services rendered to the dependents of the employees of that corporation. Before she left that office, the CEO had made a multi-million dollar pledge to Children's Hospital. That gift set the pace for other regional corporations. Many believe the Children's Hospital in Seattle, with the leadership of Mary Gates, first brought true philanthropy to the Pacific Northwest.

Then there was the combined impact of Bill Gates, Sr. and his wife Mary. They once left their young son Bill reading a book while sitting on a stool near the front desk of United Way of King County while Mary and Bill Senior gave of themselves, both in time and support, to 162 non-profit agencies affiliated with United Way of King County.

After those hallmark events brought the Pacific Northwest more fully into philanthropic activities, many other community leaders joined the new giving movement with their own personal and corporate contributions. Bill Gates, Sr. fondly remembers the charitable activities of many new, successful companies in the Pacific Northwest, with leaders who took philanthropy to heart and assumed leadership positions for local charities.

One of the most effective informational campaigns in the whole country was created by a national non-profit advisory organization called Independent Sector. Their first promotional campaign, called Give Five, was launched in 1988.

Mary Gates, along with Sam Stroum and Ned Skinner, served as board members for the Give Five regional effort from 1988 to 1992. The Give Five campaign had great media and corporate support and received over one million dollars in gifted corporate media promotion. Its message was clear and simple:

- **Give Five hours of volunteer time each week for the charitable causes of your choice.**

- **Give Five percent of your pre-tax net income each year to charity.**

Volunteering doubled in the Pacific Northwest during this 3-year campaign, and outright charitable gifts also increased dramatically during the same period.

OTHER LEADERS WHO STEPPED OUT

SAM STROUM

An early leader in personal philanthropy and the founder of Schuck's Auto Supply, Sam Stroum often raised funds for local charities. Sam loved it! One of his favorite charities was the Seattle Symphony.

Once, in a New York hotel room...on a Sunday...Sam received pledges by phone that helped balance the Seattle Symphony budget for the whole year. Later, Joe Taller, Contributions Officer of Boeing, and the Boeing Company helped Sam establish the first Performing Arts Fund in Seattle with lead gifts from Stroum and the Boeing Company.

JACK BENAROYA

A close friend of Sam Stroum, Jack Benaroya, had enhanced his estate by constructing buildings along the I-5 corridor between Seattle and Tacoma to accommodate businesses and the inventory of their products. Now people are enjoying great music in Benaroya Hall in downtown Seattle, and there are also several Benaroya Research Centers in Puget Sound.

PAUL ALLEN

As co-founder of Microsoft, Paul Allen has developed a very active family foundation specializing in gifts to universities and healthcare organizations, as well as upgrading urban areas in Seattle into state-of-the-art business parks. He has also demonstrated exceptional leadership in professional sports by taking ownership of the Seattle Seahawks football team and the Portland Trailblazers basketball team.

NED SKINNER

Ned Skinner joined Sam Stroum and Mary Gates on the Give Five volunteer board in 1989. He also started a corporate giving club in Seattle which encouraged corporations to give two percent of net corporate profits to non-profit organizations through the Seattle Chamber of Commerce. It worked well.

NORTON CLAPP

As the CEO of the Weyerhaeuser Corporation and Chairman of the Board of the University of Puget Sound for 45 years, Norton Clapp's personal gifts were large and usually anonymous. They did include irrevocable gifts to the future of the university and other favorite charities. Norton Clapp's large major gifts and trusts for charity set the tone for all major giving and planned gifts for the future in the early 1970s.

SCOTT OKI AND JEFF BROTMAN

Scott Oki, formerly an international leader with Microsoft, joined Costco cofounder Jeff Brotman to introduce the national Million Dollar Gift Club to Seattle through United Way of King County. Oki and Brotman also made their own million dollar gifts each year through United Way of King County to favorite charities, even as they personally solicited others to join the club.

DR. MARY HALL

Dr. Hall took her corporate giving expertise as head of the Weyerhaeuser Company Foundation right into the classroom of Seattle University, where she created a master's degree program for non-profit leaders.

HOWARD JOHNSON

Howard Johnson is one of the top estate planning professionals in the Northwest. He co-chaired the Leave a Legacy campaign that brought over 500 non-profits into active promotion of charitable bequests. He also facilitated a complicated large gift annuity which involved exchanging an apartment complex. The results were an exceptional gift and a delighted donor.

DOUG PICHA

Doug has led development efforts at Seattle Children's Hospital for more than 30 years. In the mid-1990s, he collaborated with his peers at 20 prominent children's hospitals in the United States and Canada to create the Children's Circle of Care – an educational and recognition program for the hospital's leading benefactors. Initially involving 500 leading benefactors, there are now more than 6,000 benefactors who have contributed nearly $4 billion over the years to advance patient care, teaching, research, and advocacy for children's health and wellbeing.

MIMI GATES

One of the recent leaders in expanding philanthropy and the arts, Mimi Gates is a past-president of the Seattle Art Museum.

Under her leadership Seattle was able to attract a spectacular traveling Picasso exhibit that was available to only three cities in America. The Picasso collection in Seattle was a huge success.

PHYLLIS CAMPBELL

Even though Phyllis Campbell has been president of two major banks in Seattle and also The Seattle Foundation, she has always given her own time generously to the communities she loves. Chairing a United Way of King County annual campaign was one of her personal gifts to the community. Another was taking The Seattle Foundation to new giving heights during her presidency of that foundation. Community leaders like Phyllis Campbell have always played a very big role in regional non-profit funding.

ED SCHUMACHER AND JANET BOGUCH

Janet and Ed are two great Northwest teachers; both recognized nationally for their clear visions of philanthropy and their fundraising experience as consultants, they were selected by the University of Washington to design and teach a "Certificated Program in Fundraising", which started in 1988. Hundreds of graduates of this very effective training program are now working as development officers at local and regional charities.

JANE CARLSON WILLIAMS

Following in the footsteps of her famous father Eddie Carlson (World's Fair leader in 1962), Jane has given great service to the whole community through her years of staff work at The Seattle Foundation. Then, after retirement, she took a leadership role in establishing an innovative, intercity school called the Seattle Girls School.

BILL GATES, SR.

When Bill Gates, Sr. was selected to head the Bill and Melinda Gates Foundation in the late 1990s, he could not wait to get to a small village in Africa where previously only a small percentage of new babies survived during their first year.

After a small improvement brought about by the Gates Foundation, the survival rate of babies in that village jumped dramatically. It was brought about because of a very simple but awesome addition to the local landscape—a new, deep well with clean, fresh water for those young babies.

BILL GATES, JR.

Excerpted with permission by Costco from *Gates on Gates*...

"A series of stunning events was set in motion two decades ago when Microsoft's Bill Gates, the world's richest man, announced plans to start the Bill and Melinda Gates Foundation, seed it with a significant portion of his personal wealth (about $27 billion), and eventually retire from Microsoft to devote full time to the foundation, which he did at age 52. The foundation became the world's largest private philanthropy. Bill and Melinda Gates' personal contribution dwarfed those of two other notable philanthropists in American history, oil baron John D. Rockefeller and steel magnate Andrew Carnegie.

In a recent conversation, the elder Gates insists there was no grand scheme by him and his late wife, Mary, to produce remarkable children. (Kristi and Libby have also both been heavily involved for decades in a variety of philanthropic and civic activities.) Instead, the mantra in the Gates household in Seattle was simply to 'show up' — whether for family life, civic activities, or school.

Mary Gates passed away from cancer in 1994. A street in her Seattle neighborhood is named after her.

A son's perspective: 'I learned so much from both my parents growing up. My parents were constantly exposing us to new ideas and encouraging us to learn, and, of course, they showed us by example.'"

Excerpted from *The Costco Connection*, May 2009
All in the Family
Tim Talevich, author

Chapter 4

WOMAN FROM PERU WALKS ALL THE WAY TO SEATTLE

"I like dreams for the future better than
the history of the past."
–Thomas Jefferson (1792 - 1826)

No one really knows how abused and maltreated the young Esperanza Rich was when she decided to leave her poverty-stricken life in Peru. Determined to make a better life for herself, she worked her way step by step through dangerous jungles, over mountains, and through deserts. She came close to death many times in her daily walks, but she persevered. Somehow she passed quickly and unheeded by the border guards in each South American country, until, like a miracle, she finally found a safe path across the southern border of the United States, into the land of the free and the home of the brave.

As Esperanza continued on her journey, despite her desperate plight, somehow she always seemed to find just the one person or a local St. Vincent de Paul charity who would always open their doors and their hearts to her, as well as their food supplies. Later she recalled the many times she received critical help from benevolent organizations along her long and painful path. Walking right up the West Coast through town after town, village by village, and St. Vincent de Paul charities, she always found help in her travels to Seattle.

After arriving in Seattle, she finally found a secretarial job at the University of Washington. Then she desperately wanted to share her meager resources with St. Vincent de Paul so others might have similar help to cross the rough pathways of life. Just before the beginning of the 21st century, Esperanza made a special gift in her will, to leave a portion of her own nominal estate to them. Perhaps she also had a hope that others would follow their own benevolent hearts and add a gift to the future in their estate plans.

Imagine her surprise when she was subsequently invited by President Bill Clinton and First Lady Hillary Clinton to join them at a conference on "Gifts to the Future" at the White House. During that conference she was honored, and her charitable bequest was featured as a model. Esperanza's response was, "I have chosen to leave a portion of my estate to one of my greatest allies during my struggle, St. Vincent de Paul. They are helping people like me every day. God bless them for what they do."

Chapter 5

John Wayne Donated Property for Marina

"I hold that man is in the right who is most
closely in league with the future."
–Henrich Ibsen (1838-1900)

On December 12, 1975, John Wayne and his wife Pilar sent a letter to the Port Commissioners of Port Angeles, Washington, announcing their intention, if accepted, to make a significant gift of waterfront property to the community. It was a complete surprise to the Port Commissioners, but one of the most exciting opportunities ever experienced in the region.

For many years John Wayne, his family, and his friends had explored the American and Canadian waters aboard his converted World War II mine sweeper, which the Duke had named the Wild Goose. Now it was clear that John and Pilar Wayne wanted to enhance boating for all families around Port Angeles and Sequim, as well as the whole state of Washington.

These are excerpts from the visionary gift letter the Waynes wrote on December 12, 1975:

"We wish to make a gift of the above-described property to the Port of Port Angeles for immediate use of the people of Clallam County and the State of Washington, including the beach frontage, the tidelands, and existing moorage and marina facilities. It is our understanding that once the gift is made the Port will be responsible for supervising, maintaining and policing the property for the benefit of the public."

JUST LOOK FOR the signs for the John Wayne Marina on Highway #101 a few miles south of Sequim.

This was the largest and most meaningful gift that the county had ever been offered by a private family. On December 18, 1975, the Port Commissioners voted to accept this generous offer and the responsibility of building and maintaining the marina. This was the start of the realization of John Wayne's desire to leave a lasting legacy of love to Clallam County and the visitors who would enjoy the facility. This particular area is considered the boating gateway to the beautiful Canadian Gulf Islands, as well as the famous fishing grounds of Desolation Sound and Alaska.

John Wayne and his family first contributed some 22 acres of prime land towards the project. More acres were added to the gift a bit later by the family, and the port bought a few more acres to complete the 39 acre project on Puget Sound. It is located just a few miles south of Sequim and Port Angeles. The higher original number of berths was reduced to 422 to ensure ecological soundness. There is a public beach, a delightful picnic area, and ample public parking. Open to the public, a five-star restaurant draws heavily from the region and attracts travelers. The Duke would no doubt get a chuckle to know that its original name was True Grits.

In the summer of 1975 my young Bailey family was exploring Canadian waters in our small 28-foot cabin cruiser named the Bailey Boat, which was usually moored near our home in Seattle. We had eventually arrived in Big Bay on Stuart Island, a remote area along Canada's western coastline where there are hundreds of inland islands and waterways. Captain Vancouver named it Desolation Sound, as he explored northwest waters searching for the illusive inland passage, which he hoped would connect the Pacific Ocean and the Great Lakes. It is a favorite salmon-fishing spot about 100 miles north of Vancouver.

As we were pulling into the dock, we had quite a surprise. John Wayne was standing on the stern of his converted Navy mine sweeper from World War II, which he had renamed the Wild Goose. His gray vessel was hard to miss, as it was 139 feet long in a narrow military style. It was not the usual run-of-the-mill fishing vessel such as those moored around it. However, here was the most prolific motion picture star of all time (142 movies) watching our arrival very closely!

I was pretty busy trying to tie up to the dock in water that can run 28 knots at tide change. But the water was quiet that afternoon, and I got help from my wife, our older son Randall, and daughter Kristin.

In the meantime, our teenage son Brad had slipped from our boat into the small dinghy that we pulled behind our cabin cruiser. He had already hooked and reeled in an 18-pound salmon, just as I was tying up to the dock.

When Brad's salmon became apparent to everyone on the dock because he was holding it up so we could see his prize, then the John Wayne persona really came to life. The Duke was conveying with his booming voice his personal observations on fishing. He mentioned things like "Paying all this money for two guide boats and skilled fishing guides to take me where the king salmon are, while a teenager like this blond-headed kid catches salmon right beside the dock!" The Duke queried the whole world with his bellowing about the intricacies of fishing and then playfully said to Brad, "Not fair, kid, not fair," while grinning from ear to ear. He kibitzed with Brad all weekend, amazed at his "unbelievable fishing skills," as Brad continued to catch salmon from our dinghy just outside Big Bay, as Duke ranted on in envy from his high-cost guide boats.

Besides the salmon events, my daughter Kristin hit it off with John Wayne's daughter who had also accompanied her father on this trip. She and Kristin, both age 13, had a great time playing together while we were moored at Big Bay. All in all, this weekend was an adventure never to be forgotten by any of my family.

But all was not well with the Duke on that fishing trip. My first clue that he was not feeling up to par came when he fired his entire crew except for his first mate. I made it a point to get next to this lone survivor that same evening and asked him what was wrong.

"Well," he said, "in the first place, the Duke doesn't like getting older. But that's not the worst part. He has already lost a lung to cancer, and he is far from well."

The John Wayne Marina was completed and opened in 1984 with the members of the Wayne family in attendance for the dedication to show homage to their beloved Duke. In 2010 its 25th anniversary was celebrated by the community and many happy boat enthusiasts. The Duke has endowed us with a wonderful lasting legacy.

Never ever have I enjoyed more the caring hearts of people like John Wayne. Since I can't thank him personally, I can only pass on my son's personal advice to him:

"Duke....in heaven when you fish, always **use fresh bait**."

Chapter 6

DR. R. FRANKLIN THOMPSON LEFT 32 LEGACIES AT UNIVERSITY OF PUGET SOUND

"As for the future, your task is not to foresee it,
but enable it."
–Antoine de Saint (1871-1944)

During Dr. R. Franklin Thompson's 31-year tenure as President of the University of Puget Sound, which is nestled amongst the evergreens in Tacoma, Washington, he was like an artist in residence, designing and sculpting 32 Tudor Gothic buildings into the campus landscape. Each one closely resembles the beautiful buildings Thompson remembered during his own post-graduate years studying for his Doctorate in Oxford, England. He loved Tudor Gothic buildings because they have a very special elegance and utility which he found absolutely captivating.

When Dr. Thompson arrived in 1941 at the College of Puget Sound (prior to attaining the status of a university) as its newest President, he had a vision. If he and his beloved wife Lucille could build a beautiful Methodist campus over the next 30 years, students would come from every part of the world to study there.

In his very first weeks at the college, Dr. T (as he became known) had a large colored artist's rendition made up of a new girl's dormitory in beautiful Tudor Gothic style. When he showed it to his academic vice-president, it took the man's breath away. "Do you really think that we can build a campus that looks like this?"

"How about one new building each year?" Dr. T responded, as he headed for his car with the rendition in his hand.

And by the end of the day he had his major gift pledge for the new girl's dormitory. And so it went.

Equally as important as those contributions to the beauty of the campus were the academic programs that Thompson and his successors have added, making UPS one of the finest independent universities in the Northwest. It is the only private institution to be awarded a Phi Beta Kappa chapter in the Northwest in 47 years.

In the early 50s when I was a student at UPS, I knew Dr. T liked to stay close to as many current and former students as possible. He had an incredible memory and knew most of the 500 students by their first names. He also had a clever way of keeping some of his alumni around after graduation or bringing them back later. From time to time he would put on a search for a few alums who he felt could help him build his beloved college and recruited them back to the campus to add strength and enthusiasm to his staff.

In the mid-sixties Dr. T was looking for alumni expertise that could help him take UPS to the next level of public recognition and into higher and more broadly offered academic programs. Before he retired Dr. Thompson had students coming from every state in the nation and 27 foreign countries. The overseas programs, Semesters Abroad, flourished so that students could both study and travel in European and Pacific Rim countries.

Dr. Thompson also understood the value of having athletic programs of excellence along with outstanding academic programs. It was Thompson's interest in expanding the role and recognition of the University of Puget Sound throughout the Northwest and nationwide that sent him into the corporate community on recruiting missions several times in the 1960s.

At the time I was aware that some of my favorite graduates were already on Thompson's staff at UPS, like Doug McArthur, first named Alumni Director and later Athletic Director. He was widely known for his superlative sports broadcasting and promotional abilities. Dr. Bob Albertson was a young faculty member at UPS who was later named one of the ten best professors in America. And then there was Joe Peyton, who was an all-American football player and an all-world charismatic individual. Thompson's right-hand man as Vice President was an alum named Richard Dale Smith, one of the best student recruiters in the country.

One day in 1965 Dr. Thompson stopped by the Eastern Washington offices of Darigold in Yakima to say hello to me. I was the Regional Retail Sales Manager of Darigold and also operated an inhouse advertising agency, with clients like New York Yankee's pitcher Mel Stottlemyre, the Washington State Fair, and of course, Darigold.

It wasn't the first time Dr. T had called on me. Years earlier I had interviewed him on our new ABC television affiliate called KNDO in Yakima. I was jack-of-all-trades, which included giving the daily weather forecasts. It was not a time of great television sophistication, and one person filled many different positions. At one point, I dashed into the TV station, ripped the weather report off the teletype, and ran over to do the weather spot, proudly announcing that tomorrow would be "fartly ploudy". I never did live that one down, and I had to answer all the phone calls questioning my prediction. Peter Jennings and I were both young men at the time, he an ABC news anchor in New York while I was messing up the weather report in Yakima.

What I didn't know was that this time the president had come to actually offer me a new position on his staff as Director of Public Relations with an eventual title of Vice President of University Relations. (Thompson also wanted my help in fundraising.) Very few ever said no to Dr. T when he turned on his Irish charm. He told me that he would get me a spot in heaven overlooking both UPS and ABC if I would come back to Tacoma and help him build our beloved college.

He convinced me I could help him raise money and awareness to build an even greater University of Puget Sound. After conferring at length with my family, I accepted his challenge.

In my new campus position, my office was right next to Thompson's office. It soon became evident that this man had a unique working style. He would meet with the faculty and staff early in the mornings and then head off the campus into the corporate community about 9:00 A. M. to make eight to ten drop-in fundraising calls until about 4:00 P. M., when he would head back to the campus to meet again with faculty and staff.

In fact, most of Thompson's fundraising calls were made alone. For instance, every year after his annual fundraising visits to local breweries, he would be waving the brewery checks in his hand as he hurried toward his office right past my office in Jones Hall. I joined him, as did his whole staff, gathering around this Irish dynamo who averaged garnering $2,500 per day in donations such as he was announcing this particular day. And with the checks in his hand, he lectured us:

> "These are large gifts from several breweries and, of course, some of our Methodist minister board members would call this TAINTED MONEY. I simply say to you
>
> > God Bless the Breweries! This money is not TAINTED.
> >
> > It just TAINT ENOUGH!"

Everyone in the local and regional corporate community loved to see R. Franklin Thompson when he walked through their doors with his latest artist's rendition of the next Tudor Gothic building he wanted to erect at his beloved university. It did not hurt fundraising to have the chairman of Weyerhaeuser

Timber Company, Norton Clapp, also heading up the UPS Board of Trustees, either. Doors opened when Mr. Clapp shared his personal enthusiasm for the educational institution he served for 45 years.

Thompson seldom made appointments, but always carried fresh Irish candy with him, and by the time he left a corporate office, they were all smiling, even when they remembered the pledge they had just made. He always promised donors a spot in heaven overlooking the UPS campus if they would just help him with this next building.

Many times I saw Dr. Thompson enter the same offices where I was reading magazines while waiting for a scheduled fundraising appointment, hoping I could get some pledges. But while I was still reading magazines, Thompson had usually worked the whole office building from the corporate offices above to the retail stores below, making a great impression wherever he went.

Dr. T was always in a hurry to get his next building started. He would raise a third of the cost before construction began, another third while the building was being constructed, and the final third when it was up and occupied.

However, even Dr. T would find a person, from time to time, who did not have a giving heart. When he made a call on someone like that, he would simply make this comment in his written report:

"He does not seem to have a benevolent bone in his whole body." Or, if there was still a chance: "He has excellent control of his benevolent emotions."

In addition to helping him raise money, Thompson also wanted my experience in television broadcasting, along with that of Doug MacArthur and Ed Bowman. He wanted us to promote UPS even further afield, and in 1966, with Thompson's full support, we launched one of the first prime time college sports series in the country. On KTNT television we featured 26 weeks of UPS football, basketball, and swimming each year over a nine year run. Each broadcast season was viewed on Saturday nights at 8:00 P. M., a rare time slot for televised sports on a regional television station.

During this nine-year televised sports adventure, we featured academic programs during the breaks in the games and slowly grew to become the largest independent university in the Northwest. We also delivered, during this period, a NCAA Division II national basketball championship under the great coaching leadership of Don Zech.

All this public awareness was possible because Dr. Thompson was so open to new promotional ideas and solid new academic and athletic programs. He even agreed that the university could be one of the major sponsors of its own television series "as long," he said, "as academic programs and excellence are promoted and the interviews are conducted with the faculty."

And that's exactly what Doug MacArthur and Ed Bowman and I did. They were the play-by-play sportscasters, and I interviewed professors about their innovative programs both here and abroad. Viewers loved it, and enrollment began to advance dramatically. How is that for integrating great academics with great sports?

I loved working for Dr. T. He taught me all the effective ways he knew to motivate people to give money to a great university, but I was particularly inspired by this Irish visionary because he had helped thousands of young men and women get a great liberal arts education.

Even though I was helpful with Dr. Thompson's fundraising effort, I was not able to add significant support for the University of Puget Sound until he introduced me to the marvelous potential for charities and any giving family through named family endowment funds, which are usually left in the family will. I will never forget the moment it happened, and then it became a continuing life-long passion of mine. Dr. T and I were on a fundraising trip in Wenatchee. As an ordained Methodist minister, Dr. T would usually preach on Sunday mornings from the pulpit of a local Methodist church. Then he would call on the most responsive parishioners that Sunday evening in their homes, with his latest artist's rendition in his hand.

It was in the spring of 1969 Dr. Thompson and I were sitting in the living room of an elderly couple. He had delivered a guest sermon at the local Methodist church that morning, and after the service this lovely elderly couple had invited us to dinner. In the course of our evening discussions, the couple opened up to share their deep frustrations. "Even though we have no children, we had always hoped to make a lasting difference at our local Methodist church. But we cannot find a sustaining way to help …any longer than it would take for the congregation to pay for new hymnals or to carpet the old chapel."

And that's when Thompson laid out the most exciting gift plan I had ever heard. (It was only proper to take into account in the equation the very modest value of their house. It had, at that time, a fair market value of $60,000.) The words and suggestions of Dr. Thompson were music to my ears and also to this delightful couple.

Dr. Thompson said, "If you were to gift your home to the University of Puget Sound, either now or when the second member of your family passes away, you could continue to live here as long as you both should live. But then, after your lifetimes, with your advance written permission, UPS would sell the house and turn that $60,000 home value into a permanently endowed scholarship fund in your names with a $3,000 annual scholarship award to a college-bound student. Furthermore, by taking only 5 percent out of your fund each year for the scholarship ($3,000 the first year), your fund will continue to grow and over time provide a scholarship fund...in your name ...every year to a Wenatchee Methodist church student going to UPS each and every year forever!

The family was stunned, and so was I. They began to tear up as they realized they could make a difference in their community in a lasting way, after all. In perpetuity is a long, long time.

At the end of his 31 years at the University of Puget Sound in 1971, Thompson was the longest serving college president in America. He had only one year when he did not erect a building, and that particular year he finished two buildings. In addition, the university attracted an enrollment that placed UPS as the largest independent university in the Northwest.

Dr. R. Franklin Thompson and Martha Pearl Jones Circa 1955

It was no surprise that Dr. T would play-act a scene with the head of the drama department, the legendary Martha Pearl Jones, who gladly shared a milkshake with the president and a passionate love affair in the silent film segment of the show called "Tillie's Punctured Romance."

Besides, "Teach Jones" was a great sport and knew that Dr. T's wife, Lucille Thompson, was also a fan of the show and the campus-wide effort to get it on stage. "Teach Jones" also gave her all for the drama and speech students and made us feel we could really open on Broadway if

GOD BLESS YOU, R. Franklin Thompson. I know you have a place in heaven overlooking your University of Puget Sound and all the lasting legacies of love you have left behind.

we wanted it badly enough. Many speech and drama grads from the College of Puget Sound did just that.

Chapter 7

SOME CORPORATIONS HAVE TAKEN A TURN FOR THE FUTURE

"The future is purchased by the present."
–William Wordsworth (1770-1850)

In the early 1970s many chief executive officers of Northwest corporations were upset with their community giving programs. Mostly, as I learned from the few CEOs I knew personally, it was because they were being solicited continually for small sponsorship gifts with very little gratitude or recognition for their donations.

One CEO of a very large regional bank was asked for sponsorships of every musical presentation in the region, but when he attended one of the concerts, he could not see any reference to the company's support anywhere in the program. Because of such occurrences, there was a general dissatisfaction among business people with their charitable donations.

In 1978 Norm Rice and Kumi Kilburn, two exceptionally bright contributions executives at Rainier Bank in Seattle, representing the corporate officers of the bank, notified all non-profit organizations in the region that Rainier Bank would be taking a complete hiatus from charitable giving until they had time to study a new concept in giving. They carefully chose their own community priorities, rather than always just reacting to community pressures. That way they were able to make charitable gifts that would bring measurable returns for both the community and the bank. They hoped that this new program would bring them more return, or at least some recognition of their contributions.

A few months later, Rainier Bank announced their first full-ride scholarship program for outstanding minority students who attended any one of the ten independent colleges and universities in Washington state. These students would also show some interest in banking as a career. The Rainier Bank Awards for outstanding minority students were, perhaps, the most successful corporate investments in education in a century of independent college/corporate partnerships.

The partnerships were clearly defined:

1) Exceptional minority candidates recruited by the colleges

2) Full-ride financial support provided by the bank

   This award not only paid for tuition and books, but also covered room and board.

3) Summer jobs and intern opportunities offered to students

4) A few full-time positions offered to graduate students

For the bank it evolved into actively helping to train talented minority students whom they could then employ in their own company.

In the decades before the 1970s, very few corporations were interested in making endowment gifts to colleges and universities. Most corporate boards of directors responsible for their own company stock portfolios did not make gifts of stock to charities. They made it clear that the primary role of long-term funds like endowments were the company's own long-term investment plans and portfolios.

Gradually, however, corporate interests began to surface for more healthful activities of colleges and university students as companies realized that future employees of a corporation must be happy and fit members of the communities where they live. That was why Seattle-based REI decided to support the proposed recreational facility planned at Pacific Lutheran University in Tacoma, Washington. This broke new ground for corporate gift possibilities. REI not only provided capital for the project, but also helped PLU endow the program and facility.

The Independent Colleges of Washington facilitated this endowment gift and were the proud recipients of a national award for supporting a new and refreshing endowment gift category. The author of this book was the president of ICW at the time and has helped identify and solicit endowment gifts ever since.

About that same time, United Parcel Service of America, a Seattle-born international company whose founder always deeply believed in the value of a liberal arts education, made a $3.5 million gift of their corporate stock to the endowment funds of the Independent Colleges of Washington. There was a restriction that the stock could not be sold on the market, but would remain in the stock portfolio of the Independent College Funds of America. Today that endowment gift is worth over $30 million at lCFA, and each year other companies join the endowment field to help train tomorrow's corporate leaders today.

NAMED CORPORATE SCHOLARSHIPS HAVE BLAZED A WIDE TRAIL

Unlike endowment gifts, where there was some reluctance, corporations have pioneered many great scholarship programs with tremendous results for the sponsoring companies and the college faculty, as well as the exceptionally talented students.

In the 1970s the Coca-Cola Company set a pace and a place in Washington that exceeded all expectations of student applicants and their families, the Independent Colleges of Washington, and even this corporate sponsor. The company had a Northwest regional office in Seattle which hired a member of the National Football League Hall of Fame (Hugh McElhenny) who became very active in assisting high school students reach their full college potential. The obvious way to attain this goal was to offer college scholarships. However, these scholarship candidates were not only the cream of the crop academically, but were also active volunteer community leaders. This type of college scholarship had not been given in the past, and it was to set the tone for rewarding well-rounded students who make a difference in their own communities. Each year Governor Booth Gardner announced the names of the recipients, as well as giving credit for all of their accomplishments, both scholastically and in their community, at a special luncheon in the Governor's Mansion in Olympia, with the parents and media in attendance. In addition to the significant financial awards to each recipient, the Coca-Cola scholarships created a tremendous list of potential future employees for the sponsoring corporation.

In the 1970s and beyond, many thoughtful corporations in the Northwest began using the objectives of philanthropy that would not only enhance their own corporation, but also improve their communities as a whole.

Historically, it has been shown that often broadly-educated students like those from liberal arts colleges make superlative corporate leaders, and they usually continue to care about their employees, as well as their communities.

Chapter 8

STORY OF CRYSTAL CATHEDRAL PRESENTS PERSONAL CHALLENGE

"Having lately had a loud call from God to arise and
go hence, I'm convinced I must not
delay any longer."
–John Wesley (1703 - 1791)

I remember almost every detail of walking into the Crystal Cathedral for the very first time on a bright, sunny Sunday morning in February, 1988. The thousands of shiny, reflective mirrors and glass panes paved the way for my family and thousands of other families who came to worship at the new Crystal Cathedral near Garden Grove, California.

As I entered the cathedral, I found the building a religious experience in itself. Above the choir and orchestra, I could easily imagine a stairway to heaven. I almost expected to see Ethel Waters walking up the golden stairs to the pearly gates, with St. Peter reaching down for her hand. I felt like I was coming home because I had been watching Robert Schuler and the *Hour of Power* on television every Sunday for years.

As the cathedral choir and orchestra finished the "Halleluiah Chorus" and Rev. Schuler approached the pulpit to introduce his special guest, Dr. Norman Vincent Peale, I realized I was in for a bonus beyond belief. Dr. Peale had an international reputation as a great religious leader, as well as a fabulous philosopher and speaker. And, at that point, Rev. Schuler was showing off his beautiful Crystal Cathedral that Dr. Peale had helped him fund several years earlier.

DR. PEALE AND REV. SCHULER MEET IN HOTEL ROOM

It seems that Bob Schuler was (and is) extremely charismatic, even when preaching from the roof of a drive-in movie house near Garden Grove. When his drive-in family brigade had grown in numbers to over 20,000 each Sunday, Schuler was desperate to find a better and more permanent location to preach. He had been trying to meet Dr. Peale for months, but a preacher from a drive-in theater was not high on Dr. Peale's priority list. However, Schuler finally got his chance to have 15 minutes with him in Peale's hotel room in Los Angeles. Schuler wanted Peale's advice on how he could raise enough money in the modest community of Garden Grove to build the first cathedral covered completely with crystalline glass over the whole structure, including a prayer tower.

As Schuler laid out his prior successes and his very personal dream of having a cathedral made of crystal erected for a weekly televised *Hour of Power*, a small gleam appeared in Dr. Peale's eye as he came to recognize one of the greatest ideas he had ever heard to extend the love of God throughout the region and the country. As he listened to the extraordinary details of Schuler's description of his glass cathedral, Peale turned to him in that hotel room and said, "Bob, don't you realize you have already built the cathedral in your heart and in your head? All you have to do is to sell every one of those panes of glass and put the donor's name on each one."

And so it was, and so it is. And now this Sunday morning with me as part of the congregation, Dr. Peale offered a magnificent tribute to the thousands of families who had bought those panes of glass.

But it wasn't until Norman Vincent Peale delivered his special message for the day that I felt he was speaking directly to me (and a few hundred other burned-out worker bees).

He said, "It is never too late for you to help with God's plans for the world. No matter how tired or burned-out you might feel, I have a fool-proof way for you to join God's army to make this a better world—and stay active by helping with God's own plans."

Then Peale laid out a blue-print for finding just the perfect role for each one in the cathedral that day, no matter what age or skill level each might have.

"I am ninety-one today," said Dr. Peale, "and I have a new mission that God has already approved. It is to help you folks find your own personal heavenly assignments, and all you need to make this work for you is a quiet beach where you can walk and think."

"Hey," I said to myself. "How did he know I'm going to Coronado and the beach for a long weekend?"

Peale went on. "On the beach think about all the things you have done and experienced in your life...and assemble them in your mind in an orderly fashion as you continue to walk and think."

"Now comes the hard part," the good doctor said. "Try to imagine ways God could use your expertise with new pathways related to your own life experiences...and in ways that could help others."

"This is the really hard part," Dr. Peale said, "because we are all guilty of flitting from one subject to another in our minds, jumping from one thing to another. But it is only through intensive, disciplined thought that we can envision new and exciting paths to serve."

So, I did all that, or at least I tried, over three days of extended beach walking and thinking. Finally, after hours of reviewing my life and every part of it, a brand new field jumped into my mind, a field I really knew nothing about; it was international philanthropy. I was so excited to have such a thought I even conceived a small consulting company in my mind. It would be called Philanthropy International.

Dr. Peale had assured us that if we would put in the time and effort in this exploration and envision a new way to use our own experiences and skills, we could send our plans and hopes up to heaven. Dr. Peale also said that he had every reason to expect that each of us would receive a very clear answer from God.

So I sent my ideas of involvement in international philanthropy up to God. I even looked heavenward and called out to him, just like Tevye in *Fiddler on the Roof*. Then I returned to Seattle with my family to get back to the work of raising corporate contributions for our Independent Colleges of Washington.

Then it happened! The very next week after returning to the Pacific Northwest, I got a personal call from Donald K. North, President of the Burlington Northern Foundation, and Chairman of the Independent Colleges of Washington.

"Dale," he said, "Ideas for expanding giving in other countries is very much a part of this foundation's long-range plans. I recently heard that the very first World Congress of Philanthropy has formed through the leadership of various American foundations and is meeting with 58 other countries in Toronto, Canada, in May to consider ways to spread to other countries the great American pastime of giving."

He continued, stating that Burlington had some serious interests in advancing this cause, but his schedule would not allow him to attend this first planning meeting. Then he blew me away by asking if Burlington would pay my way, would I be interested in attending?

The rest is history. Out of the first conference in Toronto came solid plans for a second world meeting including a four-day intensive training program to be offered to representatives of at least 78 countries in Miami in 1992. In Toronto I was asked to serve on that international board and was named Treasurer for the World Congress that successfully attracted and trained representatives of those 78 countries.

Since that international training session, the great American pastime of giving has been exploding all over the world.

Chapter 9

CATHOLIC SISTER ACCEPTS MISSION TO FOUND UNIVERSITY IN THE YAKIMA VALLEY

"The direction in which education starts a man determines his future life."
–Plato (428-348 B.C.)

To drive from Yakima, Washington, to Toppenish about 30 miles away, it is necessary to go through Union Gap, the very spot of one of the last Indian uprisings in the state in 1855.[1]

A modern day Indian uprising had occurred again in 1981, this time joined by the Hispanic community. Sister Kathleen Ross had been sent by the Sisters of the Holy Names of Jesus and Mary, a Catholic Women's Order, to shut down the continuing education courses that had been operating in the Toppenish area under the extension program of Fort Wright College in Spokane,

---

1 A few years ago the Yakama Indian Nation voted to change the spelling of their name back to that which was used in the Treaty of 1855. So, now all the Indian Nation-related words are spelled "Yakama", but the city and county are still spelled "Yakima".

which was also operated by the Holy Names Order. Leaders of the Yakama Indian Nation and Hispanic leaders pleaded with Sister Kathleen and the Holy Names Order to withhold the closure of their extension program until a community coalition of tribal and community leaders studied a remarkable plan to replace the extension courses with a four-year liberal arts college. This was happening at the same time that liberal arts colleges were financially challenged across the country and were closing at an alarming rate.

It would take a miracle to establish a college under these circumstances, and that's exactly what happened. The local Toppenish School District owned the decommissioned McKinley Grade School near Toppenish and the 20 acres on which it stood. A local family trust offered to buy and gift the buildings and property to the new college, and a permanent board of trustees was formed to oversee the new educational beginnings.

Those new beginnings were not quite as difficult. Through the education programs Sister Kathleen had developed over several years, they only had to add several other majors to form a full college program, along with the college level faculty which is so important to a liberal arts setting. Then they were ready for provisional accreditation, which they received early in 1982.

****

Sister Kathleen was in the elevator about halfway up in a Seattle skyscraper when she grabbed the hand rail to keep from falling. She had been in this building many times before, making corporate calls on CEOs who had expressed an interest in her little fledgling college buried in the middle of hop fields on the Yakama Indian Reservation. But she had never made a call like this one, and she was very nervous. The man who reached out to stop her fall also had a personal interest in the meeting and her college.

"Don't worry, Sister Kathleen. You'll knock them dead when they get a full understanding of what you have done in the Yakima Valley," said Stan McNaughton, President of PEMCO Insurance, who was already a fan of this Catholic nun's ground-breaking work in minority education. Thirty years earlier, he had also become the founder of the organization she was about to address now, requesting membership for her college.

"Remember how I handled your first call on PEMCO Insurance? When you told me the whole story of Heritage College, I then called you Alice in the Wonderland of Education."

Here was little Heritage College operating in an old grade school building gifted to the college to serve a very place-bound community where 60 percent of the residents lived below the poverty line. The diversity of the student body was largely Native American and Hispanic adults, the least likely group of all Americans to ever attend college, much less graduate.

"Do I remember, Stan? How could I forget? You have supported Heritage so faithfully."

Sister Kathleen Ross was about to tackle her most challenging audience yet, as she tried to justify requesting membership of her tiny college in this prestigious college consortium that raises and distributes annually millions of corporate dollars to the member colleges and universities. Called the Independent Colleges of Washington, these colleges received no state support to help keep their institutional budgets balanced. If Heritage could acquire membership, it would mean additional unrestricted support to keep the college out of the red, especially during its infancy.

And her audience this morning, on the forty-second floor, would be the presidents of seven other independent colleges and universities in Washington, all waiting to hear why they should offer membership in the corporate fundraising consortium to Heritage College which had only provisional accreditation and no educational track record.

Before she took center stage at this historic meeting, Sister Kathleen silently made three wishes:

1) She wished she would be able to properly present the urgency of excellent minority education at the college level to a population isolated from other opportunities.

2) She hoped her dad was listening from heaven because it was his courageous leadership in the community and his model of self-determination that had prepared her for this kind of momentous challenge.

3) She hoped the Holy Names Catholic Order knew how thankful she was for allowing her the

honor of establishing a college where there had never been a college before.

And then she spoke to the presidents and corporate board members in attendance.

"It may seem to you that our college application to this important funding system for independent colleges is a bit premature, but I can assure you that it's not premature at all, and in fact, America is a hundred years behind the original and continuing need for good education for Native American and Hispanic students, as well as other minorities. Heritage is not only catching up to that goal quickly, but finding ways to step out in front of independent higher education in the quest for well-educated minorities."

"When I was given the very sobering duty to tell the communities in the lower valley of the Yakima River that the off-campus college classes offered in Toppenish by Fort Wright College in Spokane would no longer be possible because the college was closing, community leaders, including the Yakama Nation leadership, immediately formed a task force to save their college instruction."

"And then the gifts began to come in, even without cultivation. A local family gifted Heritage 20 acres of land near Toppenish, the former McKinley grade school which had closed down, along with the other school buildings on that acreage. The Baghwan Rajneesh in Oregon had leftover portable buildings which another local family bought for us, and suddenly we had enough room to begin our unique courses."

"But then the problem of bringing people up from poor educational preparation to college level knowledge became a high hurdle that needed to be addressed. Thanks to thoughtful computer people like Bill Gates of Microsoft and Battelle Institute in Richland, we were gifted with computers and tutorial software on almost every subject a college student should have under his or her belt. The new software interacted with the students in a supportive fashion, never pointing out the mistakes to these very shy but smart students, but always suggesting other ways to get the answers needed."

"Major foundations took an immediate interest in our groundbreaking academic work, and a few funded specialized educational programs."

(Much later Heritage received recognition and support from various national foundations.)

One of the most supportive discussions imaginable followed Sister Kathleen's presentation that day in Seattle in 1981. It's too bad that she was already in the elevator going back down when Heritage and she received a unanimous vote of confidence and immediate membership in the association. This would provide her a portion of their annual corporate campaign funds which, as a six-figure sum, would help her balance the college budget for several years during their start-up period.

The reason the vote was so quick and so affirmative was the leadership position taken by several college presidents who remembered the founding of their own institutions. Father William Sullivan, the President of Seattle University at that time, took a very strong position for immediate membership for Heritage, pointing out to the others that "All of our colleges started out on a thin thread of survivability. Several of our church-related institutions moved several times just to find a permanent home. We all started somewhere!"

Then the President of the Burlington Northern Foundation, Donald K. North, pledged to give Heritage a full share of the corporate gifts for the year, "without damaging the income flow for the other schools." That meant an extra grant from Burlington, and he was happy to do it.

Several of the ICW board members and staff also joined the efforts of Heritage College to expand regional and national giving for this incredible little college which grew to university status early in the 21st century.

In 1989, Sister Kathleen again approached Stan McNaughton, the CEO of PEMCO. This time she was hoping for a corporate gift towards the first capital campaign for Heritage College. She asked if he had in his benevolent emotions as much as $10,000 for this worthy cause. But when he signed the check and gave it to her right then, she saw that it was made out for $50,000! As Sister Kathleen put it, "This is just the amount that the college needed to get through the next year without a deficit. It isn't restricted, and it is a huge vote of confidence for our work in this new endeavor. It is the most thrilling gift I have received for the college."

A few years later, the Burlington Northern Foundation, with help of others, made sure that Heritage had a fine new library. It was named by Heritage for the head of the foundation, their long-time friend Donald K. North. The Vancouver-based Murdock Foundation named the computer wing for their founder, who started the Techtronix Corporation.

****

It was in the mid-1990s that the Heritage College President Sister Kathleen Ross brought home to her campus in Toppenish, Washington, the MacArthur Genius Award ($300,000), an honorary PhD degree from Dartmouth College, and a tape of her six-minute interview by Katie Couric on *The Today Show*.

My very favorite Catholic nun was sometimes very mum about her national recognition, but after I watched her being interviewed by Katie Couric about minority education, I wanted to know more about her honorary degree at Dartmouth and the Genius Award. So I went looking for her on campus and caught up with her in the computer wing. I had good reason to talk with her, because I was serving at the time as her Vice-President for Campus Development for five years.

"Well, boss, that was a fabulous interview with Katie Couric. How did it go at Dartmouth?"

"It went well, Dale, but I was a bit overshadowed by the brilliance at Dartmouth."

"Well, I doubt that," I said. "Who got the other honorary doctorates?"

Sister looked down at an imaginary row of seats and pointed as though she were still on the graduation stage:

"OK, right beside me was Maurice Sendak and then Alexander Solzhenitsyn. Then there were one, two, three Nobel laureates ...then Elizabeth Dole and ...ME!"

Within a couple of years, Sister Kathleen had also received the governor's highest civilian award, a national committee appointment from the Secretary of Education in Washington, D. C., a publisher's award in New York, and had been named the MacArthur Foundation Genius.

Perhaps the most emotional and far-reaching story I ever observed about the first few years of Heritage College was the true story of a young Hispanic woman who earned money for her large family by picking hops in a field directly across the county road from Heritage. Each day she had to lock her four young children in her car for safety for hours while she was working. But as she was picking, she was also dreaming and hoping that someday she could become a classroom teacher, perhaps by attending Heritage College across the road. What a great dream!

One day when she had a few minutes free after picking hops and with her children in tow, she checked with the Admission Counselor, Bertha Ortega, about financial aid for working students. Bertha armed this young mother with one of the financial aid funds provided by enthusiastic donors for new teachers. She enrolled at Heritage and received financial aid, thanks to the community of donors who shared the vision of raising place-bound Native Americans and Hispanics out of the apple orchards and hop fields into the classrooms of Heritage, and then into the workforce of the community.

Today that young Hispanic mother is a graduate of Heritage University, teaching in the Yakima School District. Several of her own children are now heading toward the teaching profession. As the first member of her family ever to attend college, this lady, like many others in the Yakima Valley, has taken a phenomenal educational step upward for herself and her whole family.

The educational miracle of Heritage College, which is today a fully accredited university, has been recognized and celebrated nationally. But the real kudos have come from the Heritage students themselves. I recently met with one of the minority graduates who went on for an MBA at Harvard University. He said, "I had no problem with my advanced study at Harvard. I was well prepared for post-graduate study by the faculty at Heritage University."

No wonder the MacArthur Foundation chose Sister Kathleen Ross to receive their MacArthur Genius Award!

Chapter 10

KUMI KILBURN WAS A FUTURIST

"We make a living by what we get; we make a life by
what we give."
–Winston Churchill (1874-1965)

Kumi was sitting in a corner booth in Duke's restaurant on Lake Union when I slipped in across the table from her on that cloudy day in Seattle early in the spring of 1996. It was easy to see that she had been crying, but there was also a look of determination in her eyes that I had not seen since her divorce. I could tell that the self-reliant professional I had always admired was back in action.

I remember thinking how very proud Kumi's distinguished Korean family would have been of her, just as she had been so very proud of her own father and grandfather, chosen for leadership positions early in their lives by leaders of the Korean government. They had been sent to America to prepare for future key positions by attending America's finest universities.

Kumi's own career path in America had also been superlative. After serving on a Seattle school board as a volunteer for several years, she joined Rainier Bank. There Norm Rice, assisted by Kumi, introduced a new concept of corporate giving by objectives at the bank. After Mr. Rice decided to leave corporate life and run for public office, eventually being elected Mayor of Seattle, Kumi stepped right into his shoes as Contributions Executive for Rainier Bank in 1978. She installed it as one of the nation's strongest corporate scholarship programs. The Rainier Scholars Fund, with full rides to selected colleges and universities, had an emphasis on students of color, some of whom now have careers in banking.

So, here she was, one of the great ones in the contributions field, sharing her latest vision for Heritage University near Toppenish, Washington. Her idea was so unselfish it took me by surprise. Kumi was on the board at Heritage at that time, and I was helping them secure endowed scholarships.

"Dale," she said, "you know how much emphasis Heritage University is placing on getting more endowed scholarships. Sixty percent of the student families in the Yakima Valley are below the poverty level in income. You set up an endowed scholarship honoring your mother, one of the first Apple Blossom Princesses of Yakima. That gave me a fresh idea. I, too, would like to honor someone I love and admire. I am offering to establish an endowed scholarship in the name of Sister Kathleen Ross, the president of the college. I know that with her vow of poverty to the Holy Names Order she would not be able to fund one herself, and honoring her own personal contributions to the college, including founding the school will, for all time, be honored with her own permanent named and endowed fund."

Since Kumi had no reserve of funds to make that happen all at once, she asked Rainier Bank to forward a portion of her monthly paycheck until the entire $10,000 fund was permanently endowed. I saw tears of joy when both Sister Kathleen and Kumi celebrated Kumi's sacrificial gift.

Although many endowed funds have come into Heritage University since Kumi funded the Kathleen Ross Endowed Scholarship (about 100 at the last count), her gift to honor the founder of Heritage University remains one of the most selfless gifts I have observed in my 35 years of fundraising.

At this point in this wonderful story of creativity, selflessness, and determination, I wish I could have Kumi Kilburn take a personal bow and add a written comment. But we lost Kumi late in 2010, and much too suddenly.

So, even though Kumi is probably now on the committee to help plan the Second Coming, we are all left with only the delicious memories of a woman who will make a difference wherever she goes, even in heaven.

Three cheers, Kumi! We are all inspired by your vision!

Chapter 11

DONALD K. NORTH PRESENTED GIFTS IN UNEXPECTED AND HUMOROUS MANNER

"The future ain't what it used to be."
–Yogi Berra (1925-)

I was at the Fifth Avenue Theater in Seattle in the mid-1970s when Liza Minnelli stopped the show for ten minutes with an unbelievable performance. Another time I heard Sammy Davis, Jr. take the roof off the Tacoma Dome with "What Kind of Fool Am I?" while Frank Sinatra and Dean Martin yelled and screamed along with the rest of the audience in the early 1980s.

But neither of those show-stopping experiences compared to the stopping of a small community theater show in Eastern Washington in the mid-1980s, even before the curtain went up.

That's when one of the most creative corporate foundation presidents in America, Dr. Donald K. North of the Burlington Northern Foundation, stepped up to the ticket window of the community theater on opening night and asked to see the manager of the theater and his wife.

The cashier tried to explain to Dr. North that the husband and wife administrative team for the theater was an acting team as well, and both had parts in that spring musical show with the curtain going up in less than five minutes.

"Well, would you please just tell them that Donald K. North has come to see the show and ask if they can see me for just a few minutes?"

If they had an Olympic event for timing travel down a hallway to a dressing room, that cashier would still hold the world record, not only for the dash down, but also the dash back to tell Dr. North that "Yes, he could indeed see the husband and wife team in full makeup and costumes, right in their dressing room." He did go see them and gave them an astounding gift.

When the curtain did come up, instead of beginning the musical, the acting team informed the audience of the amazing gift that had just been given to the theater by the Burlington Northern. Dr. North was on stage with them for the grand announcement. The tears and standing ovation from the audience for many minutes was probably quite like the multiple curtain calls of *West Side Story* when Leonard Bernstein premiered it on Broadway.

You see, this inspired man who just loved giving Burlington Northern Foundation money away for great causes, had just presented the teary-eyed husband and wife team with a check that would guarantee exceptional longevity for their community theater for many, many decades.

Don North had actually earned his new position at Burlington headquarters by helping his company with proactive giving. So, even though he was a foundation employee, in his first year in Seattle, North quickly accepted invitations and joined the Board of the Independent Colleges of Washington, also headquartered in Seattle. There he put on a fundraising hat, just like the other corporate board members and college presidents, personally helping ICW raise funds for the ten independent colleges and universities in the state.

He also joined the boards of other individual charities where the Burlington Northern Foundation was investing its charitable funds. Perhaps the most dramatic example of proactive leadership was his role at Heritage College, the young college in the middle of an Indian reservation. This and other affiliations were not frivolous decisions for him. Burlington had already chosen support for independent colleges nationwide, based upon the independent colleges' contributions to society. Burlington had been providing significant support to independent colleges across the country because of their true partnerships with private businesses.

After Donald K. North was elected the Chairman of the Board of the Independent Colleges of Washington, where I was the president and professional fundraiser, I saw many more examples of why fundraising can be fun, especially if you have the pleasure of working with an inspired Burlington Northern Foundation President with a sense of humor.

For instance, during the week preceding Christmas in 1987, ICW was very fortunate to be receiving year-end corporate gifts for the member colleges because we had a matching fund challenge going on, thanks to AT&T. We could match all new gifts or increased gifts to the ten colleges if given through our consortium organization. I had hoped that the Burlington Northern Foundation would also add to their regular year-end gift to pick up on the special matching fund with a Burlington Northern increase.

However, Dr. North was not quite ready to discuss Burlington's gift that morning when I called him for an appointment. When I got to his office, he had other Christmas plans on his mind, making much of my upcoming birthday on Christmas morning. He was telling me how his whole family planned to call me on the phone and sing "Happy Birthday", which they did and have done so many Christmas mornings since!

I loved the natural humor of this wonderful corporate philanthropist and had no problem making another appointment to "talk turkey" with him about a matched increase for our foundation giving budget. But as I was backing my way out of his office with a smile on my face, Dr. North seemed to suddenly remember that he did have what he called a "small additional check" to take advantage of the match money available.

My heart began to race because it had been Dr. North and I together who had cultivated this magnificent matching fund. At one point that fall, with the special match from "Ma Bell", we were adding more than one new or increased corporate gift each week during the matching period.

Dr. North's desk looked much like mine, so I was not disturbed that he could not put his fingers right on the check he had written. But when he asked me to help him look through the papers on his desk for the check, I began to fear that he, like me, might have really misplaced the check, and so I even helped him look on the floor under his desk. At that point, even Dr. North looked worried as we ransacked his whole office for the Burlington "increased" check. He even asked me to look in the closet and waste basket!

You should have seen the grin on his face when I pulled a rumpled envelope out of the waste basket, opened it, and saw the Burlington check made out for an additional $50,000. (That's $100,000 when matched!)

That Christmas morning I sang "Happy Birthday" to myself and then enjoyed it again later with the whole North family on my phone.

As chairman of Independent Colleges of Washington through 1989, Don North eventually coaxed two non-member independent colleges to join ICW, a consortium that became so strong that it would soon lead the nation in per-college corporate support.

When Donald K. North retired from the presidency of the Burlington Northern Foundation, he left a lasting legacy of love and dedication with a great sense of humility and humor! At his retirement, it is no wonder that the Burlington Northern Company made $500,000 available for North to designate as a gift to one of his favorite charities. He quickly named Heritage College as the recipient, and they, in turn, named their new library the Donald K. North Library. This library will be in service for hundreds of years at Heritage University, and Dr. Donald K. North's own giving methodology of giving by objectives is now a permanent part of American philanthropy.

Chapter 12

SCHWEITZER AWARD GOES TO PRINCE OF LIECHTENSTEIN

"We praise those who love their fellow men."
–Aristotle (384 - 322 B. C.)

I was standing on the podium at the new World Congress of Philanthropy in Miami in 1992 to help open a four-day training session for representatives of 78 foreign countries who came to the USA to hear more about the "Great American Pastime of Giving". After the Chairman of the Rockefeller Foundation opened this extraordinary meeting and laid out the training opportunities for the next few days, he turned and introduced me as a member of the World Congress Board and treasurer of the congress event.

It was my good fortune that he wanted me to present the Albert Schweitzer Humanitarianism Award to Prince Alfred von Liechtenstein. The prince was there beside me to accept the coveted award.

The prince gratefully accepted the Schweitzer award and then gave a brief acceptance speech. Later, as we were talking together, he was very enthusiastic about what we were hearing about philanthropy. In fact, he was so taken by the possibilities, he invited me to join him in Vienna after the congress to help him encourage European car manufacturers to sponsor and support the arts. He thought that this combination would be a perfect fit. Just take a look at how foreign car makers advertise these days; that's exactly what they do now.

The growing passion for making a lasting difference is the direct result, I believe, of the growing concern we all feel about the future of our country and our world. At no time in man's 25,000 years of recorded history has there been more concern about our future.

Many religions offer wonderful expectations for continued service to mankind from heaven, but they also never overlook the importance of loving your neighbor as yourself here on earth.

The World Congress of Philanthropy, an idea whose time had come, was America's first real opportunity to introduce the rest of the world to a tradition of personal philanthropy in our country that came from the very beginning of our nation.

Chapter 13

JOE TALLER HELPS BOEING COMPANY SUPPORT INDEPENDENT COLLEGES OF WASHINGTON

"Do not go where the path may lead.
Go where there is no path...and leave a trail."
–Ralph Waldo Emerson (1803 -1882)

When I first met Joe Taller, both of us were involved with philanthropy in the Northwest, Joe as the Contributions Executive at the Boeing Company, and I as president of the corporate fundraising arm of the Independent Colleges of Washington (ICW). When Joe joined the ICW Board early in the 1980s, he was immediately recognized for having taken Boeing to one of the highest annual corporate gifts to small colleges in America.

Joe had already served as a legislator in Olympia for two terms and then was called back to be Governor John Spellman's State

Budget Director, as well as serving six years on the National Red Cross Board of Governors.

Joe Taller briefed the ICW Board members on Boeing's gift priorities and that Boeing had completed a comprehensive study of their gifts to both public and private colleges and universities in Washington state. Very soon after that, Boeing announced a major increase in annual gifts to the private sector of higher education.

Joe explained the reason to the ICW Board. Mandatory business taxation of Boeing by the state of Washington for public universities was costing Boeing over $9.00 per student, while Boeing was gifting only slightly over $1.00 for each student in our independent colleges.

BOEING EXPANDED
its annual college gifts through ICW from just over $30,000 a year to over $530,000 per year, the largest annual corporate gift in America to independent colleges.

When Boeing considered that the ten Independent Colleges of Washington, through their four engineering schools, were graduating many engineers for employment at Boeing, the wide financial disparity needed to be addressed quickly. Joe Taller took action for Boeing to do just that.

The ICW Board was very pleased when Mr. Taller was invited to represent Washington at the National Conference of the Independent College Fund of America in 1982. And when ICFA presented the award for the state with the highest per-college corporate gift income in the nation, that hallowed trophy was presented to Washington state.

In the 1980s Joe Taller and Boeing provided even more leadership in community causes. Boeing supported the efforts of philanthropist Sam Stroum to bring the arts into full activity and appreciation in the region. During his tenure in charge of Boeing contributions, their charitable donations increased from $8 million to $32 million annually.

After retiring from the Boeing Company, Joe Taller continued his admiration for and involvement with Heritage College near Toppenish. Joe and his wife Robin even established a large endowed scholarship at Heritage to honor Joe's mother.

In recent years each Washington state governor has made sure that Joe Taller continues to provide leadership for our state by appointing him for each new term to the Washington State Parks Board.

I continue to hope that there will always be dedicated people in the Northwest like Joe and Robin Taller to help keep our families and communities well protected and supported.

Chapter 14

A BUSINESSMAN INVOLVES SONS IN PHILANTHROPY

"We can only pay our debt to the past by putting
the future in debt to ourselves."
–John Buchan (1875 - 1940)

It was about 10:30 a.m. on a spring day in 1996 when Alan welcomed his two grown sons into his posh office in lower Manhattan. Alan had exciting news for his boys, and he knew that he had the best chance of catching them if he included lunch in his invitation. As the former CEO of a very benevolent major international corporation, Alan still had the keys to the contributions office where millions of dollars flowed out each year to some of the most successful charitable causes in America.

Largely because of Alan, this was a proactive corporation, always seeking ways to make lives better here and around the world, especially in the field of education. For 35 years, Alan had given great leadership to philanthropy throughout America. In addition to his work in corporate philanthropy, Alan also had helped develop one of the most successful overseas post-graduate study programs ever funded in America, sending students to

Great Britain for further study. He had himself enjoyed the honor and hard work of being a Fulbright scholar.

One of the reasons Alan was so successful in charitable work is that he had a kind heart to go with his brilliant mind. He often chuckled when he thought of the times he had followed a grant application right out into the field so he could see the charity's work for himself.

Alan liked to stay close to his sons, even though they were grown and doing well in their own fields of interest. His older son was on his way up the corporate ladder. The younger boy was a musician playing live gigs, and he often laughed when he spotted his dad at one of the nightclub tables. In fact, Alan started out his conversation with his sons on this particular day with one of his favorite stories.

"I don't know if I ever gave you two the full story of how I got so personally interested and involved in a tiny college called Heritage College on the West Coast. I should take the time to tell you the story because Heritage is exactly the reason I invited you to lunch today."

"As you know," Alan told his sons, "I helped set up a smaller foundation here in New York to target funds to some of the small independent colleges in America. Typically, these little colleges have a liberal arts core curriculum plus special programs. Small liberal arts colleges have an incredible number of graduates that make it to the top of corporations. It's this broad education that develops many skills, or as they call the outcome of such an education "Learning for a Lifetime". Whitman College out in

Walla Walla, Washington, with a student body of about 1,300, has provided many corporate presidents and other distinguished graduates like Chief Justice William O. Douglas."

"Anyway, it was after Heritage College, out in the hop fields of Eastern Washington, had been awarded two grants from our foundation that I decided I should see for myself what they are doing that is so unique. The very first day I stepped onto that campus on an Indian reservation and saw for myself the incredible progress of adult Native American and Hispanic students, I was hooked. I joined the President's Council and have been helping Heritage raise additional funds for student aid."

"So, here is what I have done. I have set up an endowed scholarship at Heritage College, not in my name, but in your two names. That means that each and every year a student will receive your award - that's each and every year, forever! This is not only to honor you two boys with a permanently named fund, but to pass on to both of you the joy of giving."

"Maybe one or both of you will someday be able to visit Heritage and meet a student recipient of your scholarship funds. But even if you don't get there, I know you will enjoy knowing that your fund is helping someone each year."

The two sons were so stunned they did not know what to say. But they did ask a lot of questions about Heritage College during their lunch. In fact, it was after lunch and when they were heading for their cars that each son thanked his dad for such a generous gift. They both said that they hoped they could develop the kind of love of community their dad so modeled.

Alan had a smile on his face on the way home. He had just planted a big seed with two members of Generation X, which is not noted quite yet for their benevolent emotion.

Chapter 15

THE NORDSTROMS MATCH FUTURE PLEDGES FOR PIKE PLACE MARKET

"The most acceptable service to God is
doing good for man."
–Benjamin Franklin (1706 -1790)

When I was initially invited in 1992 to the Nordstrom's condominium on First Avenue in Seattle, overlooking Puget Sound and the beautiful Olympic Mountains, I was impressed by the location, but even more taken by the lady who lives there.

At that time I was Director of Major Gifts and Endowment at United Way of King County, and Jeannie Nordstrom served on my Endowment Committee. She had also become a prominent leader in many King County charities, with a tremendous interest in battered women's programs as well as all efforts to help animals.

When I visited Jeannie at her home she first showed me to the room dedicated to adoptable cats and kittens. Lucky for me

I was already blessed with several cats and a dog in my family. Even though she would have been quite pleased to send one or two kittens home with me, I did promise to pass on the invitation to others. I even asked a colleague at the Pike Place Market, and she said, "Are you kidding? I already have two of Jeannie's adorable cats. You see, I have also been to her home."

Jeannie Nordstrom first met her future husband Bruce Nordstrom at United Way of King County. Jeannie was a Southern transplant serving on the staff at United Way of King County, and Bruce was the incoming Volunteer Community Chairman for one of the annual county-wide campaigns to raise funds for 162 charitable agencies in King County. No one was really surprised when Jeannie and Bruce fell deeply in love and married. Their match was surely made in heaven, and they both had very strong personal beliefs in supporting and giving back to the community. Not only did Bruce and Jeannie personally support community projects, but they made sure that the Nordstrom Company also took a leading role in community projects.

One of my favorite stories about the giving natures of Bruce and Jeannie Nordstrom came about when Jeannie called my fundraising office at United Way to get my advice on who could best help the YWCA in King County raise $29 million in just two years to build more living spaces for battered and homeless women. Jeannie was the volunteer chair for that challenging campaign. Fortunately, I knew Stuart Grover whose consulting firm had a record of successes with other non-profit organizations. He assigned his vice-president, Sonya Christianson, to the project.

She quickly brought the YWCA Board, volunteers, donors, and prospects into active roles for this fundraising endeavor. Remarkably, the campaign did reach its goal within the two-year period.

I wish I could have been a little mouse in the corner at the Nordstrom's fireside on that special night during the Christmas holidays in 1994, when Bruce surprised his wife with the greatest gift of her life: Bruce had pledged a gift sufficient to name a whole new wing of the YWCA project for Jeannie!

It really did not surprise me when Bruce and Jeannie Nordstrom decided to challenge and match charitable bequests to the Pike Place Market Foundation in 2010, continuing until the Market has sufficient endowment funds to ensure the continuing activities of four urgent community programs already underway each day at the Market. The world-renowned Pike Place Market in Seattle welcomes over 10,000,000 visitors every year, but it also provides support to homeless and low-income families at the Market in Seattle every day. (Very recently the Foundation changed its official name to Pike Market Foundation, so that change is reflected in the following description of services.)

1) THE PIKE MARKET FOOD BANK is distributing over 36,000 bags of groceries to the homeless and low-income people of Seattle each year. This downtown food bank right at the Market provides critical support to the downtown low-income and homeless community. With

the new matching program, any family with a charitable bequest of $25,000 (or more) executed in the near term, will be matched immediately, and the match, in the donor's name, will also begin its benefits immediately, long before the donor bequest matures and support doubles.

As a volunteer named Linda recently reported, "The food bank job is done each day with enthusiasm."

2) THE PIKE MARKET MEDICAL CLINIC needs endowment funds to help cover the annual costs of quality care to elderly and uninsured patients. The range of services includes primary medical care, social work, mental health counseling, nutrition and diabetes education, lab, pharmacy support, and hope.

"I don't know what I would have done if this clinic wasn't here," Clark happily reports. "Because of the clinic, I have an opportunity to become employable again."

3) THE PIKE MARKET CHILD CARE AND PRESCHOOL support allows homeless and low-income parents the time they need to find a day job and return to find their youngsters well engaged. On

SINCE THE PIKE MARKET

is an international treasure, readers may be interested in receiving more information about the endowment program by writing

Foundation Director,
The Pike Market Foundation,
85 Pike Street,
Seattle, Washington 98101

Phone 206-682-7453

Or e-mail: mktfoundation@ pikeplacemarket.org

a daily basis a typical day can be anything but typical for the kids who receive quality early education and even enjoy visits to the libraries or museums.

"Daniel loves his school at the Pike Market. I'm a single mom and can't afford to pay for the care he gets at the Pike Market Preschool. I'm so grateful." (Jennifer, mother of Daniel)

4) THE PIKE MARKET SENIOR CENTER needs endowment funds dedicated to the center to cover all the food costs of the breakfast and lunch programs plus the entire social outreach and all the engagement activities used by the center's 1,700 members for each coming year.

"You don't know how much I appreciate this place. The loneliness just melts away when I come through those doors." (Alma is one of the 1,700 members.)

Chapter 16

NOT ALL GIFTS ARE ACCEPTED AS INTENDED

"The best thing about the future is that it comes one
day at a time."
–Abraham Lincoln (1809 - 1866)

Not every lasting legacy is appreciated in the way the donor had hoped. My wife's father began flying for the Navy shortly after Pearl Harbor, and so, at times over her teen years, my wife got to live on one of the most picturesque locations in America, Coronado, just outside San Diego.

The movie *Some Like It Hot*, starring Marilyn Monroe, was filmed at Hotel Del Coronado, one of the outstanding landmarks in that area. Its charm and popularity have never diminished. Over the years my wife and I have returned to the Del several times for conferences. It's definitely one of the most memorable spots in our country.

This is exactly how the people who live in San Diego and on the Coronado Peninsula wanted to keep it. They actually enjoyed the little ferry ride to get there. They didn't mind a bit that it sometimes took a few minutes to get across from the mainland to the end of the peninsula. It was not an inconvenience but a pleasure and part of getting there, other than driving all the way around.

But politicians often see things a bit differently than their constituents. The governor at that time was Edmund Brown, and he got it into his brain that Coronado needed a bridge. Almost from the moment he first envisioned the bridge, he was committed to building it. No town meetings were held, no surveys, no open meetings when financing was discussed and decided.

Governor Brown had a towering bridge built, and it was opened in 1969. The bridge rose so high in the air that many called it a highway to heaven or the city's own roller coaster. It stands there, towering 200 feet above the San Diego Bay. I have been on this bridge many times. It is a very impressive structure, beautifully constructed and architecturally pleasing. It probably even has its share of architectural awards. It doesn't form a direct path to Coronado, but rather it has a curve. This was done so it would be high enough for all U. S. Navy ships to pass underneath it, but not too steep for vehicles to ascend and descend.

However, when I was there the last time, I noticed that the little ferry is still taking many of the people back and forth to Coronado, just because they like to do it that way. Just like always.

Shortly after the Coronado Bridge was built, Edmund Brown stepped down as governor. I don't know what he named the new bridge, but I do know what the locals who loved the ferry ride call the new towering bridge.

Oh, yes, some of the locals call the new bridge **"Edmund Brown's Last Erection**." That's quite a lasting legacy!

Chapter 17

DISCOVER YOUR CARING HEART

"Go forth to meet the future with a caring heart."
–Henry Wadsworth Longfellow (1807-1882)

- Please sit down in the quiet of your own home, complete this questionnaire created for you, and honestly answer each question.

- Take a few minutes to answer these personal and confidential questions about yourself. Elevating the joy of giving in your heart can provide a very satisfying dimension in your life.

- After you have completed and scored this questionnaire, there are suggestions as to ways of further embellishing your already caring heart.

Q. On a scale of 1-10, how do I score in emotional concern when I hear about the worldwide hunger of children? (10 is high.)

Circle one   1 2 3 4 5 6 7 8 9 10

Q. On a scale of 1-10, where do I stand emotionally on the hundreds of puppies and kittens that are put down by Humane Societies just because they have no homes?

Circle one   1 2 3 4 5 6 7 8 9 10

Q. On a scale of 1-10, how apt am I to dedicate five hours of volunteer time each week for a charity I love?

Circle one   1 2 3 4 5 6 7 8 9 10

Q. What is my excitement level for gifts to my favorite charities?

Circle one   1 2 3 4 5 6 7 8 9 10

Q. What excitement level do I have about creating a fund to honor someone I love?

Circle one   1 2 3 4 5 6 7 8 9 10

Q. What if the charity would agree to recognize this fund each year forever?

Circle one   1 2 3 4 5 6 7 8 9 10

Q. What if this named fund made a permanent annual gift, i. e. scholarship or departmental gift?

Circle one   1 2 3 4 5 6 7 8 9 10

Q. What if I could honor my whole family with one gift after my lifetime?

Circle one   1 2 3 4 5 6 7 8 9 10

Q. What if this one gift passed on the joy of giving to my grandkids?

Circle one   1 2 3 4 5 6 7 8 9 10

Q. What if the only cost of a lasting legacy is executing a will?

Circle one   1 2 3 4 5 6 7 8 9 10

Score your "Giving Heart Quotient" by adding up all your scores and dividing by ten to get your average level of interest.

GRAND TOTAL   _____

AVERAGE SCORE   _____

Scores averaging five or more reflect true benevolent emotion. Pat yourself on the back!

Scores averaging four or less reveal a heart that is well-protected from benevolent emotion and the true joy of giving.

If your score is four or less, perhaps you would take the following steps toward improving your caring heart.

> Contact your local United Way office and ask for a list of non-profit organizations who welcome new volunteers. Ask them to include each charity's information sheet.

> Select one or two charities that pique your interest and make a visit soon to see and hear more about their causes.

> If you love what you see, sign on as volunteer for about five hours each week.

> After a few months of service, fill out the questionnaire again. Compare your scores and take appropriate action!

Chapter 18

How to Do it Yourself

"'Tis not enough to help the feeble up, but to
support them after."
–William Shakespeare (1564-1616)

Some of the most exciting lasting legacies we have ever observed have come from family members who truly wanted to honor a loved one forever and followed up with their own exploration, then initiated the rather simple steps to make that happen.

Jim and Janet Smith had admired the outstanding services of a local elder care facility because Jim's mother had been a resident there for several years before her death in 2000. They cannot forget her nor the wonderful care she received. There were no wards, just neighborhoods. Most of the care was self-directed so the residents maintained their independence and dignity. Jim recalls with pleasure the times his mother came into contact with some of the 125 daycare children that provided an intergenerational bridge for the senior residents. "They came to my mother's room in little red wagons from the first floor daycare center up to the senior facilities. She really loved having those children there. It was just like a big family."

Imagine elderly grandparents, like Jim's mom, who could on any day take an elevator down to the first floor of their building and enjoy play time and reading time with the neighborhood children whose parents had enrolled them in a daycare program right inside the same building where grandparents live out their pleasant lives.

This was the emotional back-drop to Jim and Janet's interest in establishing a permanently endowed fund to not only honor Jim's mother, but to also help the elder care center continue and perhaps even expand their compassionate care. They then decided to take some very simple but profound steps to establish that fund, steps that most can take if they want to leave behind a legacy.

1) At that first meeting, they met with the center's development officer. They signed a simple form expressing their intention to establish the Jim and Janet Smith Fund. Since it was a letter of intent, it was not irrevocable and could be adjusted or even cancelled later.

   There is now an irrevocable pledge agreement which was created and tested by Dr. Frank Minton, 115 NE 100th St., Suite 300, Seattle, WA 98125. The form is at the end of this chapter, and it is titled "Pledge Agreement."

2) A few months later, Jim and Janet executed, with the help of an attorney, an attachment (codicil) to their will which named a specific percentage of their estate that will be set aside, after both Jim and Janet have passed away, to establish the Smith Family Fund at their favorite elder care center.

3) Typically, a named family fund is handled just like a permanent savings account in a bank trust department or at a community foundation. A portion of the income each year is allocated to the charity. (For Jim and Janet Smith, it is 5 percent of the total fund balance each year.)

   Example: A $25,000 named family fund will produce about $1,250 in good investment times. That amount would be gifted to the designated charity after the first full year of its establishment and each year thereafter. When endowment funds earn more than 5 percent in their investments, most named family funds make ever-increasing gifts over time.

4) After the Smiths executed their charitable bequest and with specific instructions on how Jim's mother will be honored each year, in addition to how the funds will be expended at

the care facility, they live in the knowledge that, without spending any of their current income, they will have established a lasting legacy for their family as well as the care center.

IN ALL CASES consult your own attorney.

5) Last but not least in this chain of events, because the Smiths know that their plans may be an inspiration to others who also might want to honor a family member with a permanent family fund, they are allowing the care center to share this story with others. This is done merely as a demonstration of how very easy and fulfilling it is to leave a legacy for the future as part of an enlightened estate plan.

DEFINING CONDITIONS AND THE VALUE OF A FAMILY ENDOWMENT FUND

The definition of a permanently named family endowment fund is best understood when compared to a savings account in a bank. However, this named charitable family fund called an endowment fund has charitable intent, and only the yearly net income can be used for specified charitable causes.

(Before the current recession, endowment funds could usually deliver 3 to 5 percent of income for charitable purposes each year.)

There is nothing very complicated about setting up a planned giving program at a non-profit organization or as a donor who wants to leave a lasting legacy honoring a family and funding the future of a favorite charity.

AS A FAMILY OR INDIVIDUAL DONOR:

• Contact your favorite charity and ask what minimum gift would be required to establish a permanently named and endowed family fund and what purposes are open for the annual designation of the named fund income. Ask for that information from the charity in writing, as well as the annual written plans for family recognition, reports, and donor site visits.

• Enter legalzoom.com on your computer and find the free working document that will help you prepare the legal terminology for a last will (e.g., "Washington State Will").

- At the end of this chapter is an irrevocable pledge agreement which was created, tested and authorized for use by Dr. Frank Minton, a leading planned giving expert located in Seattle. Take a copy of this attached form with you when you go to your own attorney to execute your charitable bequest. If your bequest actuates an immediate match by your charity, this special pledge agreement makes your future bequest eligible for that match now. You may enjoy an immediate named fund put to work for your favorite charity now, with your bequest adding to the fund after your lifetime.

- Share all this information with your family members as well as the exact name of your proposed fund and the specific designation for the fund income each year. (In naming a permanent fund, you could honor a revered member of your family, use the family name, or someone else you admire.)

- Take your preliminary will text to an estate planning attorney and have the will legally drawn and executed, including the other designations of assets and properties.

• Give a copy of the will to each affected family member and keep one copy in your own safe-deposit box.

PLEASE FEEL FREE to copy and use the following forms as needed.

• If an outright gift secures your permanent fund, be sure of the ways it can be funded and with what types of assets.

• Then have a family celebration for *Leaving Yourself Behind*.

ENDOWMENT PLEDGE FORM

NAME OF CHARITY   _____

NAME OF DONOR   _____

DONOR STATEMENT:

I am adding _____ to my estate plans for the sum of $ _____ ($25,000 or more).

MY LONG-TERM COMMITMENT WILL BE IN THE FORM OF:

- ☐   A Charitable Bequest
- ☐   A Charitable Trust
- ☐   Real Property
- ☐   Paid-up life Insurance
- ☐   Personal Property
- ☐   Other assets (described in attachment)

At the time of my legally executed estate plan I understand that I will immediately receive a dollar-for-dollar match from your Challenge Fund to establish the permanent _____ Fund, a fund that will be enhanced by my own estate plans when they mature.

DONOR SIGNATURE AND DATE: _____

I understand that _____ will report about the use of those funds directly to me annually. I also authorize you to recognize my gift by name and to include my family in all recognition events and listings of similar gifts and provide us with immediate membership in your Lasting Legacy Society.

Please send your reports and the society's invitations to the following members of my family:

(FULL NAMES AND RELATIONSHIP ALONG WITH ADDRESSES, PHONE NUMBERS AND E-MAIL ADDRESSES)

_____

_____

_____

_____

_____

_____

SIGNED THIS DAY _____

NON- PROFIT PRESIDENT _____

PRINCIPLE DONOR _____

PLEDGE AGREEMENT

In consideration of my interest in benefiting [name of charity], I, [name of donor], pledge and promise that, in addition to the contributions I have already made to [name of charity] prior to the date of my execution of this agreement, I will contribute to [name of charity] between the date of my execution of this agreement and [end of date range] a total of $_____. I further pledge and promise that any portion of the $_____ I have not contributed to [name of charity] by the date of my death shall become a debt owed by my estate to [name of charity], thereby obligating my estate to distribute such portion of the $_____ to [name of charity] subsequent to my death; provided that the amount of such debt shall be reduced, dollar for dollar, as a result of any contributions made to [name of charity] – which contributions are specifically designated to be in partial or complete satisfaction of this pledge – subsequent to my death through my will, through a living trust I may have created, or through any retirement plan I may have established.

All amounts received by [name of charity] in fulfillment of this pledge shall be for [specify the particular fund, campaign, or other purpose].

This agreement in no way limits my ability to make additional gifts to [name of charity] for other purposes during my lifetime or by will or other instrument effective subsequent to my death.

I acknowledge that [name of charity]'s promise to use the amount pledged by me and/or [name of charity]'s actual use of the money pledged by me for the purposes specified above shall constitute full and adequate consideration for the pledge.

This pledge is to be irrevocable and a binding obligation upon my estate.

This agreement shall be interpreted under the laws of the State of [either charity's state of domicile or donor's state of domicile, as determined by legal counsel].

Executed this _____ day of _____ 20___.

Donor's Signature: _____
[name of donor]

Witness' Signature: _____
Printed Name of Witness: _____

CONSENT OF SPOUSE

In the event I have a joint or community property interest in any property subject to the foregoing Pledge Agreement, I hereby acknowledge and consent to the pledge of [name of donor] under that Agreement.

Spouse's Signature: _____
[name of spouse]

Witness' Signature: _____
Printed Name of Witness: _____

ACCEPTANCE

The undersigned, being a duly authorized officer of [name of charity], does hereby accept the written pledge.

Date: _____   _____
[Name and Title of Appropriate Person]

WILL LANGUAGE

I give to [name of charity] of [city and state], for [specify the particular fund, campaign, or other purpose], the sum of $ _____, reduced, dollar for dollar, by any contributions made by me at any time on or after [date pledge agreement was executed], which contributions are specifically designated to be in partial or complete satisfaction of the pledge that is the subject of the Pledge Agreement executed by me on _____ for the benefit of [name of charity], whether such contributions are made directly by me, through some other provision in this will or any codicil hereto, through a living trust I may have created, or through any retirement plan I may have established.

Chapter 19

CHARITIES CAN CREATE LASTING LEGACIES FOR DONOR FAMILIES

"While I crawl upon this planet, I think myself obliged to do what good I can in my narrow domestic sphere."
–Lord Chesterfield (1694- 1773)

- Invite a professional to explain the value of endowments to your board, your fundraising staff, and your endowment volunteers.

- Staff and board enter three-month pre-planning for the campaign.

- Name an endowment committee of 5 or 7 leaders. (See list of responsibilities following.)

- Plan and publish an overall endowment work plan and timetables.

- Submit endowment plan to the full board for approval, including campaign expenses.

- Include the terms of your new Lasting Legacy Society to the board, and include the yearly recognition program for each family.

- Solicit a challenge grant from major donor(s) willing to match irrevocable bequests or outright gifts of $25,000 of more.

Form a special committee of board members and community leaders willing to make solicitation calls with staff. Send out newsletters about the new Lasting Legacy Program. Share your new program through the mass media. If the bequests are well executed and irrevocable, the donor should receive an immediate named fund through a matching grant, and then a bequest from their own estate will be added to their fund at their death.

Stewardship begins immediately with reports to donors and continues with a yearly recognition event and a personalized memento of their lasting legacy for each donor.

ENDOWMENT CAMPAIGN

Launch a new program to encourage endowment gifts. Appoint an endowment committee (5 or 7).

1)   Agency president, acting as chair

         a. Selects a board member as vice-chair

         b. Selects a planned giving specialist

         c. Appoints financial vice president to committee

         d. Appoints a planned giving officer to staff

2)   Board ratifies above selections.

THE ENDOWMENT COMMITTEE DUTIES

1) Oversees the work of the staff and campaign volunteers

2) Reports quarterly to the executive committee and full board

    a. Progress of matching fund
    b. Bequests that will qualify for immediate match

3) Helps identify endowment programs to be targeted

4) Creates gift acceptance policies and gives to board for approval

5) Reviews all forms of endowment gifts to see if qualified for matching fund

6) Assists staff to cultivate and solicit matching funds and bequests

7) Invites committee members to consider their own bequests

8) Reviews the recognition and stewardship programs and helps raise funds to support these efforts for the Lasting Legacy Society members

STAFF DUTIES

1) Selects and purchases planned giving brochures

2) Writes the new endowment plan and publicizes it

3) Publishes and distributes gift acceptance policies

4) Identifies and solicits major challenge grant(s)

5) Announces and launches endowment campaign

6) Establishes Lasting Legacy Society (donors)

  a. Hosts annual recognition events for donor families

  b. Provides on-site donor recognition plaques

PLEASE FEEL FREE to copy and use the following forms as needed.

  c. Honors legacy donors with special tributes

  d. Prepares annual donor financial reports

ENDOWMENT PLEDGE FORM

NAME OF CHARITY _____

NAME OF DONOR _____

DONOR STATEMENT:

I am adding _____ to my estate plans for the sum of $ _____ ($25,000 or more).

MY LONG-TERM COMMITMENT WILL BE IN THE FORM OF:

- ☐ A Charitable Bequest
- ☐ A Charitable Trust
- ☐ Real Property
- ☐ Paid-up life Insurance
- ☐ Personal Property
- ☐ Other assets (described in attachment)

At the time of my legally executed estate plan I understand that I will immediately receive a dollar-for-dollar match from your Challenge Fund to establish the permanent _____ Fund, a fund that will be enhanced by my own estate plans when they mature.

DONOR SIGNATURE AND DATE: _____

I understand that _____ will report about the use of those funds directly to me annually. I also authorize you to recognize my gift by name and to include my family in all recognition events and listings of similar gifts and provide us with immediate membership in your Lasting Legacy Society.

Please send your reports and the society's invitations to the following members of my family:

(FULL NAMES AND RELATIONSHIP ALONG WITH ADDRESSES, PHONE NUMBERS AND E-MAIL ADDRESSES)

_____

_____

_____

_____

_____

_____

SIGNED THIS DAY   _____

NON- PROFIT PRESIDENT   _____

PRINCIPLE DONOR   _____

PLEDGE AGREEMENT

In consideration of my interest in benefiting [name of charity], I, [name of donor], pledge and promise that, in addition to the contributions I have already made to [name of charity] prior to the date of my execution of this agreement, I will contribute to [name of charity] between the date of my execution of this agreement and [end of date range] a total of $_____. I further pledge and promise that any portion of the $_____ I have not contributed to [name of charity] by the date of my death shall become a debt owed by my estate to [name of charity], thereby obligating my estate to distribute such portion of the $_____ to [name of charity] subsequent to my death; provided that the amount of such debt shall be reduced, dollar for dollar, as a result of any contributions made to [name of charity] – which contributions are specifically designated to be in partial or complete satisfaction of this pledge – subsequent to my death through my will, through a living trust I may have created, or through any retirement plan I may have established.

All amounts received by [name of charity] in fulfillment of this pledge shall be for [specify the particular fund, campaign, or other purpose].

This agreement in no way limits my ability to make additional gifts to [name of charity] for other purposes during my lifetime or by will or other instrument effective subsequent to my death.

I acknowledge that [name of charity]'s promise to use the amount pledged by me and/or [name of charity]'s actual use of the money pledged by me for the purposes specified above shall constitute full and adequate consideration for the pledge.

This pledge is to be irrevocable and a binding obligation upon my estate.

This agreement shall be interpreted under the laws of the State of [either charity's state of domicile or donor's state of domicile, as determined by legal counsel].

Executed this _____ day of _____ 20__ .

Donor's Signature: _____
                            [name of donor]

Witness' Signature: _____
Printed Name of Witness: _____

CONSENT OF SPOUSE

In the event I have a joint or community property interest in any property subject to the foregoing Pledge Agreement, I hereby acknowledge and consent to the pledge of [name of donor] under that Agreement.

Spouse's Signature: _____
                            [name of spouse]

Witness' Signature: _____
Printed Name of Witness: _____

ACCEPTANCE

The undersigned, being a duly authorized officer of [name of charity], does hereby accept the written pledge.

Date: _____   _____
                                                      [Name and Title of Appropriate Person]

WILL LANGUAGE

I give to [name of charity] of [city and state], for [specify the particular fund, campaign, or other purpose], the sum of $ _____, reduced, dollar for dollar, by any contributions made by me at any time on or after [date pledge agreement was executed], which contributions are specifically designated to be in partial or complete satisfaction of the pledge that is the subject of the Pledge Agreement executed by me on _____ for the benefit of [name of charity], whether such contributions are made directly by me, through some other provision in this will or any codicil hereto, through a living trust I may have created, or through any retirement plan I may have established.

Chapter 20

SOLID GIFT ACCEPTANCE POLICIES ARE ESSENTIAL

"It is our future that lays down the
law of our today."
–Frederic Wilhelm Nietzsche (1844-1900)

Perhaps no single aspect of gifts to the future is more important to charities than clearly defining the kinds of gifts acceptable to the board of directors and the government well before they are gifted. This preplanning is even more important when dealing with either unimproved or improved property, as well as personal treasures like art objects and personal items. All these are difficult to appraise and sometimes have long-range problems that are attached to such acquisitions, such as meeting government requirements for a tax deduction.

This author once observed an expensive piece of recreational property being offered to a Seattle charity at a suggested gift value based on the values of other comparable recreational properties. However, the missing element of this potential outstanding gift for the charity was that the original property owner and developers had not conducted an environmental study. Since this situation had all the elements of a nightmare, the Seattle charity wisely stepped away from the gift.

A few charities across the country have actually gone under by accepting marginal gifts and then being unable to satisfy the governmental requirements for environmental studies on gifted properties.

REFERENCES FOR FURTHER INFORMATION

Washington State Bar Association (online)

- Ask for list of Estate Planning Attorneys in your region

- Free Washington will forms online

- Write a legal will online

Planned Giving Services, Seattle

- Frank Minton, PhD, President, expert on planned giving

- 115 NE 100th St. Suite 300, Seattle, WA 98125

Legal Zoom.com (online)

- Offers many legal services at economical costs

The Seattle Foundation (online)

- Offers management services for family foundations

United Way of King County (online)

- Offers training for charitable volunteers

- Offers list of King County charities and their goals

Philanthropy International, Dale Bailey, President

- Specialist in Endowment Funding

- (360) 412 1666

- 6814 Fairway Lane SE, Olympia, WA 98501

NOTES